SHADOWS AND THE DARK

John Cowburn SJ

SHADOWS AND THE DARK

The problems of suffering and evil

SCM PRESS LTD

334 01498 0

First published 1979
by SCM Press Ltd
58 Bloomsbury Street, London WC1

Typeset by Gloucester Typesetting Co. Ltd
and printed in Great Britain by
Billing & Sons Ltd
Guildford, London and Worcester

CONTENTS

Introduction   vii

Part One: Extreme Optimism and Pessimism
1   Optimism   3
2   Pessimism   14

Part Two: A Moderate Optimism based on Evolution
3   Evolutionary Optimism   23
4   God's Responsibility and Our Own   31
5   Criticism of Evolutionary Optimism   39

Part Three: Moral Evil: its Nature and Cause
6   Moral Evil   45
7   The Content of the Morally Evil Act   51
8   The Mystery of Evil   61
9   God and Sin   75
10 The Wages of Sin, and the Thesis of this Book   82

Part Four: The Remedy for Moral Evil
11 Repentance   97
12 Forgiveness   103
    Conclusion   116

    Notes   117
    Index   131

INTRODUCTION

This book is for thinking Christians who are intellectually puzzled and emotionally affected by the disorders of our world, and who wonder whether they should accept them or take action to remedy them. They may also be troubled in their faith in God. What I offer is mainly an intellectual view, but account is taken of emotions, including anger, and of action. It is an obvious mistake, and one typically made by philosophers, to imagine that when one has explained the nature and origin of evil one has completely solved 'the problem of evil', as if it were nothing but a logical puzzle; but it is equally a mistake to dismiss the intellectual problem as remote from life or insoluble, for sense must be made of life if we are to cope with it emotionally and engage in efficacious action.

The view which I shall present supposes that there are two kinds of unorder or disorder. In making this division I shall not put 'physical evil' on one side and 'moral evil' on the other; rather, on one side I shall put troubles that are no one's fault, and on the other side I shall put moral evil and the troubles, including the physical disorders, that follow from it, so that (for instance) some cases of sickness are on one side of my division and other cases are on the other. I shall say that the difference between these two kinds of unorder or disorder is so radical that each is a problem in its own right, and hence we have not one 'problem of evil' but two problems. To the first problem I shall present a solution in terms of an understanding of evolution after the manner of Teilhard de Chardin. It involves positions which resemble those of process theology, but is not simply identical with them; and if it involves a review of the concepts of divine omnipotence, omniscience and providence, it does not include an outright denial of them. In dealing with the second problem I shall examine the morally evil act as a phenomenon in human experience, and here I shall draw on works of literature as well as philosophy and theology. Of course, Macbeth and the characters in *The Brothers Karamazov* never existed; but Shakespeare and Dostoyevsky, and other authors whom I shall quote, had a deep knowledge of people and they expressed this in their works. For instance, into *Macbeth*, *Othello* and other plays Shakespeare put the results of his thinking about what goes on in the minds and hearts of men and women who commit extremely evil deeds. These works, then, are not sheer fantasy but pictures of real life as these writers saw it: as such they can be quoted here. I shall also quote Karl Barth and some other evangelical theologians, which is a somewhat unfashionable thing to do now. It is my belief that these theologians were deeply right in the passages which I shall quote from them about sin, and the appeal to fashion – which has replaced the appeal to authority as the weakest of arguments – will not invalidate their insights.

Some very important questions are not discussed here, including the following: in what sense death is an evil, and the implications of personal immortality; whether there will be an existence of our world beyond the extinction of life on this planet, if that is going to happen; whether punishment is ever a remedy for evil; whether expiation is needed, as well as repentance and forgiveness, for the complete healing of guilt; whether the devil is a real person; and how Jesus saved us from sin by his death and resurrection. That is to say, the solutions which I am going to present are not completely worked out: they are the beginnings of solutions. Also, while some account is taken of other views – indeed, the first two chapters are entirely devoted to other views – this book is not intended to include a complete survey of theories about evil; and while references are made to some current controversies, such as that between libertarians and determinists, no attempt is made to enter into them.

Finally, this book is not, I hope, morbid. If it hurts to read some of its pages, as it hurt to write them, it is my hope that the end result will be a degree of intellectual clarity, appropriate emotions, and confidence in action: in a word, my aim is not to hurt but to heal.

PART ONE

EXTREME OPTIMISM AND PESSIMISM

1

OPTIMISM

Many Christians have believed that God's control of events is so complete that of everything that exists or happens we must say: 'God planned this in advance; it is his will.'

Here and there in the Bible a writer shows that he has come to the conclusion that a seemingly chance event was planned by God. In Genesis, when God is said to be in haste to cause Egypt to have some good seasons followed by some bad ones, seemingly random variations in weather are attributed to God; there is no apparent design in the way people fall in love, but when Samson falls in love with Delilah this is said to be 'from the Lord, for he was seeking an occasion against the Philistines' (Judg. 14.4); and when Tobit is blinded in what looks like an unlucky accident, he calls this being scourged by God (Tobit 11.15). There are even places where the evil deeds of men are said to have been willed and brought about by God: Joseph is wickedly sold into slavery by his brothers, but later says, 'God sent me before you to preserve life' (Gen. 45.5) and even, 'It was not you who sent me here, but God' (45.8); Peter says that when Jesus was put to death God was carrying out what he had foretold (Acts 3.18); and the apostles pray as follows: 'There were gathered together against thy holy servant Jesus, whom thou didst appoint, both Herod and Pontius Pilate, with the Gentiles and the peoples of Israel, to do whatever thy hand and thy plan had predestined to take place' (Acts 4.27–28).

In later Christian writings the idea is more fully worked out. It is the basic thesis of the 'Treatise on Conformity to the Will of God', by Alphonsus Rodriguez, whose *Practice of Christian and Religious Perfection*, published in 1609, used to be prescribed daily reading for Jesuit novices and many other religious. It was preached by eighteenth-century English divines like John Clarke and Soames Jenyns. Indeed, it came to be widely regarded as self-evident that the Christian God must totally control all events in advance, and this has been re-stated recently by Professor Geach, who says:

> God is the supreme Grand Master who has everything under his control. Some of the players are consciously helping his plan, others are trying to hinder it; whatever the finite players do, God's plan will be executed. . . . God cannot be surprised or thwarted or cheated or disappointed.[1]

The immediate inference from this is that everything that happens is for the best. 'All things that happen,' said Wyclif, 'turn out to be the best things that may be. . . . This world is made better by everything that happens in it.'[2] What seem to be calamities, said Rodriguez, prove in the end to be beneficial.[3] Soames Jenyns explained how wrongdoing produces good effects: 'Robbery may disperse useless hoards to the benefit of the public; adultery may bring heirs, and good humour too, into many families, where they would otherwise be wanting; and murder free the world from tyrants and oppressors.'[4] Milton said:

> All is best, though we oft doubt
> What the unsearchable dispose [disposition]
> Of highest wisdom brings about,
> And ever best [is] found in the close.[5]

And Alexander Pope put the doctrine into rhyming couplets for people to memorize:

> Respecting man, whatever wrong we call
> May, must be right, as relative to all.
>
> All nature is but art, unknown to thee;
> All chance, direction, which thou canst not see;
> All discord, harmony not understood;
> All partial evil, universal good,
> And, spite of pride, in erring reason's spite,
> One truth is clear: 'Whatever is, is right.'[6]

This, of course, is the optimism which Voltaire satirized in *Candide* and which ever since has been called 'Panglossian'.

Sertillanges expressed a basic principle of this optimism when he said that the more all-embracing our view of reality is, the less evil we see[7] – with the implication that if our view could be utterly all-embracing, we would see no evil at all. This is some-times expressed in analogies. Life, it is said, is like a tapestry which we see from behind: it looks chaotic, and while if we stand back far enough we may be able to see the blurred suggestion of a pattern, when we look at details we see only untidy loose ends; but if we could see the tapestry from in front, where God is, we would realize that nothing is out of place in it and that what we see from behind is just as it ought to be. Or else it is said that life is like a musical composition. Turning the knob of your wireless set some day, bringing in stations and immediately tuning them out again, you might happen to hear a second of dissonance and say, 'What a cacophony! Something has gone wrong there.' But it might be a moment from a great symphony, and those listeners who were hearing the work from beginning to end would know that the sound which displeased you had to be made at that point, or was right. Finally, it is said that the world is like a clock. If you look at the pendulum or balance wheel you see it swinging or spinning endlessly back and forth, back and forth, and you may be tempted to say: 'This is absurd. If it belongs on the left or right, it should stay there. If it belongs in the middle, it should settle there.' If, however, you understand the working of the clock as a whole, you know why the pendulum or wheel must move as it does and you find its movement wholly admirable. This makes it clear that the optimist's answer to the problem of evil consists in the assertion that there is no evil, or that it is a sort of optical illusion.

According to this view, tragedies are basically false, and many writers who think that optimism is part and parcel of Christianity have said that 'no genuinely Christian tragedy can exist',[8] that religious drama, 'by the nature of some of its basic assumptions, cannot be tragic',[9] or that 'there is no room within the Christian thought-world for the idea of tragedy in any sense that includes the idea of finally *wasted* suffering and goodness'.[10]

Whatever theologians may say of it today, this optimism is still a component of Christian folk-wisdom, and it is often used to cope with death. If, for instance, a young man has died in a car accident, the preacher at his funeral may say: 'To unbelievers our brother seems to have been the victim of blind chance, and his death seems an absurd waste; but we who have faith know that God's providence watches over us at all times, we know that our brother has died because God chose to call him to himself at this time, and therefore we know that our brother's death came at the right time for him. Though young, he had completed his course.' It is also used to cope with suffering. I once broke my leg, and when I was in hospital a religious said to me, 'You must have needed a rest.' She had obviously said to herself: 'God wanted him to break his leg, otherwise it wouldn't have happened; therefore it was beneficial for him to break his leg. How could it be? Perhaps he needed a rest, yes, that must be it' – and here she spoke aloud to me – 'you must have needed a rest'. The reasoning is applied to all the suffering in the world heaped into a great mass of pain. It is affirmed to be God's will, and therefore for the best, and the question, 'How can it be?' is answered by saying that suffering provides opportunities for charity, that from it come great works of art (Beethoven may be mentioned), or that without suffering there would be no spiritual growth, life would be boring, and we would all be taking drugs for lack of other stimulus. When the same reasoning is applied to the sin of Adam, the result is called the myth of the Fortunate Fall, according to which the Fall of man was a Good Thing in the long run, so that we should all give three cheers for Adam and sing, as a medieval poet did:

> Blessed be the time
> That apple taken was
> Therefore we must sing
> Deo gratias.[11]

It is now time to show not that this world-view is false – that is obvious – but how bad it is.

First, if we were to apply it to our own actions it would make us irresponsible, at least, for it implies that it is impossible for anyone to make a bad choice and that therefore when we have to make a difficult decision we can say to ourselves: 'Whatever happens is right; whatever I do, I will know once I am doing it that it is the best course of action; therefore I can spare myself the trouble of collecting information, weighing alternatives, seeking advice, agonizing; I can simply do the first thing that comes into my head, or whatever I happen to feel like doing, and rest secure in the knowledge that I have made the right choice.' This cannot be right.

Secondly, 'whatever is, is right' would make a fine motto for an ultra-conservative's coat of arms. 'People are dying of starvation?' he might say. 'If so, that is God's will and it is right. We are very rich and others are very poor? It is God's will and we must accept that. So should they.'

Thirdly, this world-view implies that in making a prayer of petition we are either asking God to do something which he is going to do anyway, or else we are asking him to do something which he certainly will not do and which we should not want him to do; that is, in this system of thought prayers are either pointless or bad, and we should not make them.

Fourthly, the theory seems incompatible with the existence of moral evil. Some people see this, and from the proposition that everything that happens is God's will they deduce that no one ever formally sins. This makes nonsense of much of the Bible; it implies that when Christ said, 'Let him who is without sin among you be the first to throw a stone' (John 8.7), they could have all let fly; it thins life by whisking out of it all struggles of conscience, pains of guilt, and dramas of repentance, forgiveness and reconciliation; it takes all substance out of the ideas of salvation and redemption; it implies that tragedies like *Macbeth* are fantasies that have no relation to real life, whereas fictions in which everyone is good are true to life; in short, it embodies a pathetically glossy, untragic view of human existence, and to assert it is to be like the monkeys who cover their ears and eyes and 'hear no evil, see no evil'. Also, while it may lead one to be super-charitable in one's judgment of other people's actions, it has bizarre implications if one applies it to one's own, for it means that if one covets one neighbour's goods or wife one may go ahead and take them or her, it will not be a sin. It is more usual to reconcile the theory with the existence of moral evil by distinguishing between God's efficacious and permissive wills. God, it is said, does not directly will or personally cause sins to be committed; he does, however, refrain at times from preventing sins from being committed; and he does this only when he sees that good rather than harm will result from them. Augustine said that evil 'would not be done if he [God] did not permit it (and surely his permission is not unwilling, but willing), nor would he who is good permit evil to be done unless in his omniscience he could turn evil to good';[12] Journet says: 'If evil was not permitted for the sake of a good, the action by which God permits it . . . would be perverse';[13] and Geach says that wicked men have their place in the divine order of things – 'Extreme villainy', he says, 'is the necessary means to produce such virtue as that of Thomas More or Maksymilian Kolbe. . . . God allows the villainy in order to have the virtue.'[14] It is thus admitted that sins are committed, and nevertheless it is maintained that God is in total control of the universe and that all events in it – even sins – are for the best.

However, not only does a good end not justify *doing* something immoral; it does not justify *wanting someone else to do* something immoral in the future, or *being glad someone else has done* something immoral in the past. If I say, 'I believe it would be immoral to kill a certain person (I have in mind a certain world leader), but I wish someone would do it, for the sake of peace in the world', I commit sin; and if it happens and I am glad, knowing that I am being glad that someone has done wrong, I commit sin. In the view outlined in the preceding paragraph God does not, perhaps, make people commit sins (this is the point of the efficacious/permissive distinction); but he does want people to commit sins either because of good consequences they will have or because of what they will give him the opportunity to do, and this is wrong and therefore impossible. Moreover, this is simply not God's attitude towards sin as shown in the Bible. When, for instance, the Israelites commit idolatry, does God say to himself: 'Good, everything is going according to my plan, and good will result from what they are doing down there', and merely pretend to be angry? Surely the dominant teaching of the Bible is that God in no way wants people to sin. Evil deeds and their consequences, then, are *not* willed by God, and we do not have that ground for supposing that they are for the best in the long run.

Moreover, if this theory were valid, how could we repent of our sins? Milton's Adam had this problem, and he said:

> Full of doubt I stand
> Whether I should repent me now of sin
> By me done and occasioned, or rejoice
> Much more, that much more good thereof shall spring –
> To God more glory, more good will to men
> From God.[15]

Also, when tempted to commit a sin we could say to ourselves: 'It may be wrong, and at a superficial level an offence against God: but if I do it I will know that God planned it, and is permitting me to do it because he sees that good will come of it, so that at a deeper level I will be pleasing him by carrying out his design.' Again, this cannot be right.

Fifthly, while some minor or medium-sized troubles turn out to have been blessings in disguise, great disasters render total optimism incredible. One such disaster was the Lisbon earthquake of All Saints Day 1755. At about half past nine in the morning there was a rumbling noise and a trembling of the earth, followed by a pause. Then the earth shook for two minutes, bringing down buildings and doing other damage. After a second pause, there was another shock, which did further damage. By this time the air was thick with dust from the rubble, and no one could see what was happening. A quarter of an hour later this dust was beginning to settle, and it was seen that fires had broken out. These spread. The waters of the Tagus became agitated and began to rise. At half past ten or eleven o'clock an after-shock did serious damage in the western parts of the city, and brought down a church in which people had taken refuge, while seismic waves of water broke over the quays and foreshore and did damage there. In the course of the morning thousands of people were crushed and hundreds were burned to death. This occurred at a time when it was 'in' to believe that 'whatever is, is right' and that 'all is for the best in this best of possible worlds', and as the news spread through Europe people were stunned by it. Within a short time, some men said that the earthquake had been willed by God and was a blessing. In Portugal, a certain friar preached and later published a 'consolatory sermon' in the form of an address given by Jesus to the Portuguese people, in which he told them that they should be proud to have been singled out as they had been by being given it. A Jesuit preached along similar lines and made himself a nuisance to the civil authorities, because whereas they were trying to get the city rebuilt as quickly as possible, he said that by means of the earthquake God had told people to turn their minds away from the things of this world and give themselves entirely to prayer. (He, poor man, was later found guilty of heresy and publicly strangled.) But others felt that optimism had been convincingly refuted.[16] And surely no one with a Christian idea of God could believe that in accordance with a design or plan God *wanted* the slaughters of World War I or the torture, gassing and burning of six or more million Jews in the Nazi period, that he *wanted* the Vietnam war to be waged, and that he wants what is now happening in Northern Ireland to go on (assuming that it will continue.) Also, when the father or mother of young children dies, and the preacher tells the congregation that he or she died at the right time, this is more than the immediate family can believe; and when a boy or girl becomes a heroin addict, the parents cannot believe that 'whatever is, is right'. Vatican II said that man 'is engulfed by manifold ills which cannot come from his good Creator',[17] and in those words denied the basis of the unqualified optimism which so many people still think is essential Christian doctrine.

Sixthly, the optimistic world-view contains within it a quite horrible idea of God. I have already shown that in so far as it maintains that God wants immoral things to be done, it implies that he is immoral. It also implies that he is ruthless. This point is made at length in *The Brothers Karamazov*, where Ivan says to Alyosha: 'If you were planning the universe, and you could give men peace and contentment in the end by torturing to death one little girl, would you do it?' No, he implies, you would not be so ruthless; but God is.[18] If someone goes blind or deaf, or both, or contracts some crippling and painful disease, then according to this theory he is in the universe like the brake-lining in a car, which is essential for the perfection of the car as a whole but is subjected to terrific heating and grinding. God would have to be ruthless indeed to use persons like this.

Finally, for those who believe in it, hell is the final refutation of total optimism. It has been argued that hell is necessary to show the justice of God, or to enhance the joys of heaven;[19] but the idea that God planned in advance that some people would go to hell, because he judged it would in the long run be a good thing (though not for them, obviously), is surely utterly unacceptable. And consider the following passage, about a child in hell:

> The little child is in this red-hot oven. Hear how it screams to come out. See how it turns and twists itself about in the fire. It beats its head against the roof of the oven. It stamps its little feet on the floor.

The writer carries on in this vein for a while, then says:

> God was very good to this little child. Very likely God saw it would get worse and worse, and would never repent, and so would have to be punished much more in hell. So God in his mercy called it out of the world in its early childhood.[20]

This is not even logical; if God could cause a child to die before it could commit *worse* sins and have to be punished more, he could cause a child to die before it committed any sins, in which case it would go to heaven, and obviously if he was going to be 'very good to this little child' he should have done that. But psychologically it is even worse. The author of that passage was surely a sadist, who gloatingly described the child in pain and relished the thought of the agony he was going to cause his readers to suffer, and he pictured God as a sadist like himself. Something horrible that is implicit in the 'optimistic' system, but usually hidden, comes out of hiding in that passage.

This is why, when people have had this optimism taught to them as Christian doctrine and then in adult life encounter great suffering, they have religious crises. They may, like Père Paneloux in Camus's *The Plague*, force themselves to will the suffering because God wills it, making a superhuman effort 'to believe everything, so as not to be forced into denying everything';[21] or they may reluctantly decide they can believe no longer, for 'if there were a God these things would not have happened'. They may go through a period of still believing in God but being angry with him, or even subconsciously hating him; and a few become anti-theists, putting themselves among those

> Souls who dare look the Omnipotent tyrant in
> His everlasting face, and tell him that
> His evil is not good![22]

It has to be granted that when people are in distress the optimistic view can console them momentarily, by assuring them that what seems a mere random occurrence has been rationally willed, that what seems meaningless is part of a plan, and that what seems bad is in the long run for the best. It is the after-effects that are frightful. For instance, people whose child has died have been consoled at first when told that God has taken their child to himself for their and its own good; but afterwards the words 'God has taken your child from you' have rung in their ears and the crisis has occurred.

Let us look at two more moderate views of evil. The first of these is that its existence is adequately explained by the Principle of Plenitude, which can be presented in this way; it is wonderful that mankind has great masterpieces like Chartres cathedral, the Bach B Minor Mass and Shakespeare's tragedies; but our artistic heritage would be strange and incomplete if it consisted only of major works like these, and we need to have works like the Mozart quintets and *The School for Scandal*, which are minor masterpieces, and we also need trifles like Schubert's waltzes and *The Importance of Being Earnest*; similarly, for the universe to be complete it needs to have not only very great beings, but also minor beings and beings of trifling significance. This is the Principle of Plenitude, and those who think it explains evil go on to say: 'and bad things'.[23]

There is a fallacy here. The world is the richer for having Schubert waltzes as well as the B Minor Mass, for having *The School for Scandal* as well as *Othello* and for having Ronald Searle cartoons as well as the paintings of Velasquez; but all these works are good. The world is not the better for the *bad* works it contains: on the contrary, it is polluted by them. Similarly, to have a full human life a man should experience times of great happiness, and also smaller satisfactions such as those that come from seeing the sun come out after rain or unexpectedly getting a shot in at tennis; but it would be absurd to say that it is good to have a full life and this must include some experiences like being unable to have children, being sent to prison, going mad, committing murder or being killed when young. Evil is not lesser goodness and therefore the Principle of Plenitude cannot be used to justify its existence.

Plotinus, Augustine and Thomas Aquinas proposed a theory of evil which seems at first glance to be cheerful, because it reduces evil to nothing. It can be stated as follows. Light and dark may at first appear to be like two opposing forces, but in truth light is energy and darkness is nothing. Similarly, good and evil may seem to be two opposite forces, locked in an eternal conflict, as the Manicheans believed; but goodness is being and evil is the lack of being. Blindness, for instance, is a physical evil and it is the lack of sight. These thinkers set out to show how all evils turn out on analysis to be as it were holes in being. Scholastic philosophers go on to say that the will's object is always being, and therefore good; hence evil can be produced only as a side-effect – 'the direct term of an action is never evil' and 'evil as such is never willed'.[24]

This, however, is less cheerful than it sounds, because the fact remains that the holes in being are there, that there are many of them and that some are enormous. The fact that non-arms are non-being does not make armlessness any the less distressing. Also, the theory cannot convincingly be fitted to moral evil, for deliberate murderous violence is not lack of gentleness, and hate is not lack of love; moreover, the evil in them is willed directly.[25]

What is true in this view is the idea that evil is essentially a derived or secondary thing. If we say that a painting is bad or that a person has something wrong with him, it is because we have at least approximate ideas of what paintings and people normally are and by referring to these have seen that something is missing from or does not belong in the particular painting we are talking about. Similarly, if we say that something is wrong with the engine of a car we are thinking of how it ought to run. We can, however, think of what is normal without having to refer to what is defective: if a man wants to learn how a car engine works he studies one that is in good working order and need not refer even mentally to broken-down engines. As for moral evil, this is essentially destructive, and as such cannot be a primary reality for it necessarily presupposes something to be destroyed. As Ricoeur says, 'however *radical* evil may be, it cannot be as *primordial* as goodness';[26] or, as Berkouwer says, 'Evil has no thesis in itself but only antithesis'.[27]

PESSIMISM

At the other extreme, there is utter pessimism.

There is, firstly, the view that there is no inherent pattern or design in the universe, or certainly not in the things that happen to people. Events follow each other, sometimes bringing good to persons and sometimes bringing bad, without any reason. Moreover, whatever we say, do or become will ultimately be swept away, so that in the end nothing really matters. Life, in this view, is in the end

> a tale
> Told by an idiot, full of sound and fury,
> Signifying nothing[1]

and the world is 'a senseless and detestable piece of work'.[2] James Thomson wrote:

> The world rolls round for ever like a mill;
> It grinds out death and life and good and ill;
> It has no purpose, heart or mind or will.[3]

In Somerset Maugham's *Of Human Bondage*, Philip – who stands for Maugham himself – realized that

> there was no meaning in life, and man by living served no end. It was immaterial whether he was born or not born, whether he lived or ceased to live. Life was insignificant and death without consequence. . . . What he did or left undone did not matter. Failure was unimportant and success amounted to nothing.[4]

Bertrand Russell wrote:

That Man is the product of causes which had no prevision of the end they were achieving; that his origin, his growth, his hopes and fears, his loves and his beliefs, are but the outcome of accidental collocations of atoms; that no fire, no heroism, no intensity of thought and feeling, can preserve an individual life beyond the grave; that all the labours of the ages, all the devotion, all the inspiration, all the noonday brightness of human genius, are destined to extinction in the vast death of the solar system, and that the whole temple of Man's achievement must inevitably be buried beneath the debris of a universe in ruins – all these things, if not quite beyond dispute, are yet so nearly certain, that no philosophy which rejects them can hope to stand. Only within the scaffolding of these truths, only on the firm foundation of unyielding despair, can the soul's habitation henceforth be safely built.[5]

An even gloomier view than this one is that the universe is inherently destructive, malign, vicious, vindictive or in a word evil. According to Ricoeur, Greek tragedy embodied an idea that could not be openly expressed – that the gods who rule the world are wicked, or in more secular terms that there is an inherent malice or guiltiness in being.[6] Una Ellis-Fermor writes of 'Satanic dramas' in which it is implied that particular evil events are but manifestations of the inherently evil nature of the universe: Marlowe, she says, 'did not question the nature of the world-order. He saw it steadily and saw it evil.'[7] In Shakespeare's *Troilus and Cressida*, she says, the existence of a principle of order in the cosmos and in human affairs 'vanishes, revealing destruction as the principle underlying all life'.[8] This play, she says, implies that the only absolute is evil.

Baudelaire said that in discussions of evil one always comes back to Sade; to the Marquis de Sade, then, we now come. Until the eighteenth century, optimism was generally based on belief in a benevolent personal God; then men moved from theism to deism and began to talk of 'God or Nature', and then just Nature, but the benevolence of the personal Christian God was carried over and attributed to the unpersonal deity and then to Nature, so that optimism survived. At this point Diderot and others became doubtful about their optimism, for what rational basis was there for believing Nature to be ethically good and benevolent to man? Sade now entered and

said: I just look at nature; I put speculation aside and accept
the evidence – 'I bow to evidence only, and evidence I perceive
only through my senses; my belief goes no further than that,
beyond that point my faith collapses.'[9] And when I look at
nature, he went on, 'is there any limit to the injustices we see her
commit all the time?' I see how animals live, and how savages
in a state of nature live. I observe that man's inborn and hence
most natural impulses are violent and lustful. And I say: Take
Nature for your guide, imitate her, do what she impels you to
do, yield to your passions which are the means Nature employs
to attain her ends:

> Must we not yield to the dominion of those [inclinations] Nature
> has inserted in us? . . . Were Nature offended by these proclivities,
> she would not have inspired them in us; that we can receive from
> her hands a sentiment such as would outrage her is impossible,
> and, extremely certain of this, we can give ourselves up to our
> passions, whatever their sort and of whatever their violence,
> wholly sure that the discomfitures their shock may occasion are
> naught but the designs of Nature, of whom we are the involuntary
> instruments.[10]

This means that to be true to Nature we should do many things
that are now regarded as crimes. If Nature could talk she would
say to us:

> Idiots, sleep, eat, and fearlessly commit whatever crimes you like
> whenever you like: every one of those alleged infamies pleases me,
> and I would have them all, since it is I who inspire them in you.
> . . . If there exists a crime to be committed against me it is the
> resistance you oppose, in the forms of stubbornness or casuistries,
> to what I inspire in you.[11]

In Nature, argues Sade, there is no love or kindness, and so
these ought to be sedulously avoided. 'You mention, Eugenie,
ties of love; may you never know them!' For 'nothing is more an
egoist than Nature; then let us be egoists too, if we wish to live in
harmony with her dictates'.[12] The wolf who devours the lamb
acts according to Nature, and the man who understands nature
'no longer fears to be selfish, to reduce everyone about him, and
he sates his appetites without inquiring to know what his enjoy-
ments may cost others, without remorse'.[13] Sade takes the

reasoning a stage further when he argues positively for cruelty to others. 'Cruelty, far from being a vice, is the first sentiment Nature injects in us all.'[14] Savages are cruel until civilization teaches them kindness, thus rendering them unnatural – 'Cruelty is simply the energy in a man civilization has not yet altogether corrupted; therefore it is a virtue, not a vice.'[15] And in sexual experiences, for a man's pleasure to be greatest it is 'very essential that the man never take his pleasure except at the expense of the woman'.[16]

So far, what Sade has done is to maintain as devoutly as any-one before him that Nature is the ethical norm, and then deduce from that an ethical code which is the reverse of the generally accepted one. At this point he is saying, in effect, that Nature is good, Nature is cruel, therefore cruelty is good. However, he now changes his ground and says that Nature is inherently, profoundly evil. He writes:

> A God exists. A hand has created all I see, but for ill. . . . It is in evil that he created the world, it is by evil that he keeps it in being, it is for evil that he perpetuates it, it is impregnated with evil that the creature should exist, it is to the womb of evil that it returns after its existence is over. . . . I see eternal and universal evil in the world.[17]

He concludes that we ought to do evil, and his heroes and heroines hurl themselves into evil, seen as evil. A woman cries out:

> Oh, Satan, one and unique god of my soul, inspire thou in me something yet more, present further perversions to my smoking heart, and then shalt thou see how I shall plunge myself into them all.[18]

Another character says:

> Oh, what a pleasure it is to destroy! . . . I know of nothing more deliciously enjoyable. There is no ecstasy like that which one enjoys when one gives oneself up to this divinely infamous action.[19]

And after Juliette has been practising vice for the enjoyment of sexual and other pleasures, Madame de Clairwil requires of her that she purify her motives and do evil 'solely for the pleasure of doing it'.

That is one way of living in a world that is meaningless or even malevolent. There are others.

Some people, seeing the world like this, fall into despair and say with the chorus in *Oedipus*: 'I call none happy who beholds the light', or 'Not to be born at all were of all things the best; but, if born, then to die as soon as possible.'[20] They say:

> This life itself holds nothing good for us,
> But it ends soon and nevermore can be;[21]
>
> This little life is all we must endure,
> The grave's most holy peace is ever sure;[22]

and they commit suicide or are kept living only by a biological drive that they do not have enough strength of will to resist.

Others live from week to week, giving themselves to people they love, dedicating themselves to work, accepting from other people and from life the good things they offer, and simply not letting their minds dwell on ultimate questions which (they say to themselves) are unanswerable, anyway. *Candide* ends on this note, with Martin saying: 'We must work without arguing' – that is, without speculating – 'that is the only way to make life bearable', and Candide saying: 'We must cultivate our garden.'

Others seek a solution in art. Nietzsche writes that man sees the horribleness and absurdity of being and is nauseated. Also, he sees that action is useless. At this point, Nietzsche says, art approaches to save him. As only she can, she twists his insights into representations with which he can live; the sublime, which is the artistic subjugation of the horrible, and the comic, which is the artistic discharge of the nausea caused by the absurd.[23]

Yet others maintain their dignity and achieve a certain nobility by defiance. In 'The Free Man's Worship' Bertrand Russell urged man,

> undismayed by the empire of chance, to preserve a mind free from the wanton tyranny that rules his outward life; proudly defiant of the irresistible forces that tolerate, for a moment, his knowledge and his condemnation, to sustain alone, a weary but unyielding Atlas, the world that his own ideals have fashioned despite the trampling march of unconscious power.[24]

Some authors maintain that this is the essence of tragedy. In a tragedy, they say, and I agree with them in this, something goes wrong for a man not because of some purely contingent circumstance but because of some deep if dimly perceived necessity: we miss the meaning of Lear, for instance, if we think that the establishment of adequate homes for old people would solve the problem.[25] The tragic hero, these authors go on to say, defies and resists this necessity even as it crushes him, and so remains great, sublime in his fall. The greatness of his opponent is greatness of physical power. His own greatness is greatness of spirit.[26] Thus tragedy 'shows human effort to be sublime, a fit match for the sublimity of nature and nature's gods'.[27] 'Tragedy exalts man in our eyes.'[28] The tragic attitude, according to this view, is expressed in exemplary fashion by Anouilh's Antigone and by the old rabbi in Maxwell Anderson's *Winterset*, who says:

> and Mio – Mio, my son – know this where you lie,
> this is the glory of earth-born men and women,
> not to cringe, never to yield, but standing,
> take defeat implacable and defiant,
> die unsubmitting.[29]

Finally, some people simply live in contradiction. On the one hand, they believe that nothing has meaning or value; on the other hand, they live and act as if some people or things do matter. One of Faulkner's characters says:

> You get born and you try this and you don't know why only you keep on trying it and you are born at the same time with a lot of other people, all mixed up with them, like trying to, having to, move your arms and legs with strings only the same strings are hitched to all the other arms and legs and the others all trying and they don't know why either except that the strings are all in one another's way like five or six people all trying to make a rug on the same loom only each one wants to weave his own pattern into the rug; and it can't matter, you know that, or the Ones that set up the looms would have arranged things a little better, and yet it must matter because you keep on trying or having to keep on trying and then all of a sudden it's all over.[30]

Pessimism has a strange appeal, but, firstly, it is totally irreconcilable with Christianity. Secondly, if *in the long run* nothing has lasting value or meaning, then *in the last analysis* there can be no morality and even the torture of a child does not finally matter. As Camus says,

> If we believe in nothing, if nothing has any meaning and if we can affirm no values whatsoever, then . . . the murderer is neither right nor wrong. We are free to stoke the crematory fires or to devote ourselves to the care of lepers. Evil and virtue are mere chance or caprice.[31]

Moreover the pessimistic theory of tragedy is not verified by many of what are indisputably the world's great tragedies. Shakespeare's tragedies, for instance, suppose not that the universe is absurd or even malign but rather that it has a certain order or rightness: and they do not glorify the defiant shouting of 'No' to being. Those who maintain that defiance is the essence of tragedy usually go on to say that therefore there can be no Christian tragedy; but great tragedies are affirmative to a degree that is irreconcilable with sheer pessimism. It is not Christianity but pessimism which excludes tragedy.

PART TWO

A MODERATE OPTIMISM BASED ON EVOLUTION

3

EVOLUTIONARY OPTIMISM

It is a fact of observation that all living things have life-spans; their existence begins at some point in time, and they are then tiny; they grow to maturity in a matter of days, if they are insects, or years, if they are human beings; then they go into decline and eventually die. During their period of maturity they reproduce themselves, so that as they pass beyond their maturity another wave of beings of the same kind reaches it; thus the species endures. It also seems that non-living things have existence-spans: mountains rise up, then are worn down; stars are born and eventually burn out; everything has a beginning and proceeds first upwards, then downwards and out.

It has been scientifically demonstrated that as beings are replaced, increasingly complex beings appear: at one time there were only simple molecules in existence, then some complex ones appeared, then living things, then more and more highly developed living things, then very primitive human beings, and development went on until it reached the human beings who exist today, such as we are.

I wish now to propose a philosophical postulate: that to exist in this way, with a life-span or more generally an existence-span, and with gradual progression in time from lower beings to higher ones, is of the nature of material beings, so that it would be impossible for them to exist in any other way. That is, I am postulating that it would be inherently impossible for corporeal living beings to exist which never developed nor declined physically, so that it would be impossible to tell by physical examination whether one of them was a few years or a few centuries old; and that it would be impossible for living beings to succeed each other indefinitely, generation after generation, without progress or regression, so that however much one knew about the beings on the earth at any time it would be impossible to tell, by observing their physical state and their culture, even approximately when that time was.

Let us be clear about the kind of impossibility that is meant in the above statement. There is *logical* impossibility: it is that of a square circle, the last digit of the square root of two expressed as a decimal and a moral being who does not have free will. Some authors write as if this were the only kind of inherent impossibility, but it seems to me that a rational being existing in our universe and having the dimensions of a sphere one millimetre in diameter, and a being which has reason but not will, may not be contradictions in terms and hence logically impossible, but nevertheless are intrinsically impossible; also, there may be no logical impossibility in the idea that the universe began five minutes ago, our brains having been created then with memories of events that never occurred, but it is nevertheless intrinsically impossible that this happened. I am not saying that a non-evolving universe is logically impossible; I am postulating that it is in another way inherently impossible.

If this postulate is accepted, then at least to some extent the order and unorder in the world can be explained.

First, some of the unorder in our world, or some of our troubles, exist because the universe still has a long way to go before it is perfect. Our nervous systems are not altogether matched to our circumstances: if pain is part of an alarm system, it is anomalous that we feel pain when good is being done to us at the dentist's, and none when harm is being done to us by X-rays; it is also a defect in us that men sometimes panic and become incapable of thinking and acting coolly when their very survival depends on their keeping their heads. Also, at present we have almost no control over the weather, and little ability even to predict it far in advance, and consequently crops sometimes fail unexpectedly and food shortages or even famines occur. Moreover, people suffer and die of cancer because while we now know a great deal about the body and how to cure many of its ills we have not found the complete remedy for that. Furthermore, we have not yet evolved perfect arrangements for living and working together, so that there are always men unemployed or doing futile jobs. We do not yet have perfect systems of government at every level, from a world government through national governments to local governments; we do not have a perfect monetary system; our educational systems are imperfect; our transport systems are inadequate; and so on. Moreover, our understanding of morality is imperfect: looking back into the ancient world we are shocked by the widespread acceptance of slavery and polygamy, but we may be sure that some things we do, which are generally accepted, will be seen by later generations to be immoral – for instance, later generations may be amazed when they consider how few people would now say that it is immoral to marry for money or social prestige. These troubles can be explained by saying that we are at a certain stage of the development of the human race, with distance still to go.

Secondly, if a town which needs a hospital does not build one from the foundations up but, instead, converts an old school into a hospital, the result is never a perfect hospital; and evolution has involved many conversions like that. The first animals to appear on land had not been designed as air-breathers but were modified fish, and while further modifications have made us better adapted to air than the first animals to breathe it were, we are still fish out of water. Similarly, when animals first adopted an upright posture they did not get bodies freshly designed to stand and move in the new way; instead, they carried on with their interior organs hanging from their skeletons in a way that was more suited to the old horizontal backbone than to the new vertical one, and that is how we still are. Also, just as a hospital that was once a school has things in it that served a purpose when the building was a school but are now useless, so we have organs like the appendix which we have inherited from evolutionary predecessors and which are useless to us. That is, evolution explains what looks like bad design in nature.

Thirdly, it seems that progress can be made only with trouble or at the cost of some suffering.

Evolution seems to have taken place through random mutations and natural selection. That is, in a particular species gene mutations occurred from time to time in a random way, with the result that there appeared on the scene beings with some completely new characteristics, never before seen in members of the species, which they were able to pass on to their offspring. More often than not the new characteristics put these beings at a disadvantage in comparison with others of their kind, and the new strain died out. Now and then, however, a mutation gave rise to a new sort of being which had an advantage over its fellows, with the result that the new strain flourished and became a new and more highly developed species. Now if by the nature of the case evolution had to proceed in this way, then it was necessary that from time to time animals appeared that because of gene mutations were miserable freaks, hopeless contenders in the struggle to live. No particular being of this kind had to come into existence; but in general the appearance of such beings was necessarily involved in evolution.

In a somewhat similar way, when a major scientific or technological problem exists (for instance, that of finding the cause and cure of cancer), many different approaches have to be tried, and teams of scientists go to work, each exploring a particular avenue. Each team hopes to be the one that solves the problem and wins fame. Perhaps after they have all worked for many years, one team, partly through brilliance but also partly through luck, hits the target, publishes the solution, becomes famous and may be awarded a Nobel prize. The other teams feel that their efforts, and the money they have spent, have led to nothing, and in a way that is true; but that waste, and their disappointment, are part of the price that the human community has to pay for scientific advances.

Again, many young people study music with the hope of one day becoming famous as singers or solo instrumentalists. There is room for no more than a few at the top of the profession, so that it is known beforehand that only a few can achieve this success. The disappointment of the many who fail to reach the height to which they aspired is the price that has to be paid for the relatively few great musicians who appear in each generation.

There is another way in which progress causes suffering, and in which almost every step forward that mankind has taken has caused some suffering. The human race spread over the globe in a series of migrations, and in each of these the pioneers went into environments in which they encountered conditions to which they were not adapted, so that many died. When slavery was ended in eighteenth-century England, this was progress, but an immediate result was misery for many black people in England; and the ending of colonial regimes has brought poverty to many good people. Suffering, it seems, is the price of progress, and this same hard law operates in the Christian churches. In the Catholic Church, for instance, developments in the liturgy, theology and ecumenism have been steps forward, but there are Catholics who, when they go to Mass now, cannot pray privately in their old way because there is no silence at Mass any more, or in the new way, either, because they do not understand it, so they just suffer; and there are corresponding people in the other churches. We must face the fact that progress always causes suffering, and see that if we were to make it a rule never to do anything that would upset anyone we would never do anything – and this, in the end, would cause even more suffering. At the same time, this must not be made an excuse for riding roughshod over people, saying that you cannot make omelettes without breaking eggs; let us drive as hard a bargain with nature as we can, and seek to buy our progress at the lowest possible cost.

Teilhard de Chardin saw this clearly. In 1917 he said that 'in all evolution we have to reckon with failures and mistakes':[1] in *The Phenomenon of Man* (1938) he said that 'nothing is constructed except at the price of an equivalent destruction';[2] and in 1942 he said of the suffering in the world that in the light of evolution 'the immense travail of the world displays itself as the inevitable reverse side – or better, the condition – or better still, the price – of an immense triumph'.[3]

A person who has grasped evolution, then, sees that things go wrong for men and women. He sees children suffering and dying; he sees young adults dying and leaving husbands, wives and children whose lives are thereby at least in some degree spoiled. He sees human beings who have been cripples since birth or who are mentally retarded. He sees many people unable to find work which satisfies them, failing to find marriage partners, or marrying and discovering that they cannot have children. He sees what the total optimists refuse to face, namely that in everyone's life something is as it ought not to be. He sees this, but evolution enables him to understand it.

For centuries, the predominant explanation of evil was the reverse of this one. A state of perfection *behind* us was postulated, whether in a spiritual world, in the Garden of Eden, or in some other paradise, and to explain our present ills it was supposed that some kind of Fall or slide occurred (for Plato, it was the fall of the soul into matter; for Genesis, the fall of man from innocence into sin; for Plotinus, the slide as from God proceed lesser beings, from these still lesser beings, and so on); whereas the evolutionary theory postulates a state of perfection *ahead of* us, and a Rise towards it. The 'Rise' theory was foreshadowed by Irenaeus, who said that the first human beings were analogous to babies and that just as a mother has adult food but cannot give it to her baby because the baby cannot receive it, so God had perfection but could not give it to the early human beings because they were incapable of receiving it.[4] It appeared in the second half of the eighteenth century, when the static optimism characteristic of the earlier part of the century gave way to an optimism based on the idea of progress.[5] In the nineteenth century the idea of evolution joined that of progress and Darwin's discoveries gave great support to the theory. In this century Teilhard de Chardin worked out the 'Rise' theory in more detail, and it is more or less his view which I have been expounding.

The extreme optimist believes that every event in the universe happens according to a minutely detailed plan. Some pessimists believe that there is no plan at all. The evolutionary or Teilhardian optimist believes that there is an overall pattern of growth, but that many particular events are unplanned and unpredictable.

First, many random events occur. An event is random if, at some stage prior to its occurrence, it could either occur or not occur, and no person decides whether it is to occur or not. Such events are to be found in the reproduction of living beings. It is in a highly random way that the pollen of any particular plant fertilizes some other particular plant, and it is only slightly less a matter of chance which animal mates with which other animal; there is an immense overproduction of germ cells, most of which are lost, and it is a matter of chance which ones survive and give rise to new plants, though in any particular instance this determines which genes are passed on to the offspring; plants release huge numbers of fertilized seeds to be scattered by the wind, of which most die while some by chance land in places where they take root and grow. In human beings, too, it is a matter of chance whether in any particular instance a child is a boy or a girl, and which particular combination of genes it inherits from the millions which are possible. In short, nature is not like a clock in its operations connected with reproduction; it works through randomness. [6] Random events are also to be found in the activity of molecules, atoms and particles. In a gas, molecules move at random, and in a radioactive substance it is a matter of chance whether a particular atom emits an alpha particle in the next minute or in over a hundred years time. Also, during wars, guns or mortars are sometimes fired not at particular men but in the general direction of the enemy. It is then a matter of chance whether one man is hit or another. Since it is shocking, even humiliating, to recognize that if one is killed it will be by sheer chance or bad luck, men sometimes tell themselves that for each man who is going to be killed there exists beforehand a particular bullet which has his name invisibly on it: until it is fired, he is safe; when it is fired, he will be hit; if there is no such bullet he will survive the war. Thus necessity replaces chance – in fancy, not in fact. In all these cases, the event is not predetermined: prior to its occurrence, it is possible that it will happen, and it is also possible that it will not happen (or it is possible that it will happen at a particular moment, and possible that it will not happen at that moment). Now if we assume that a true statement cannot turn out to have been false, then if someone says 'The event will occur', this cannot be a true statement because it is possible for the event not to occur; and the statement 'It will not happen' cannot be true, either. That is, it cannot be true to say 'It will happen' or 'It will not happen'; the event, then, cannot be predicted with certainty. The most that is possible is prediction with probability, and it may be possible to give the probability a numerical value.

Secondly, human beings perform free acts. In saying this, I am assuming that determinism is wrong and that human beings have free will. Let me explain by an example what I mean by this. Suppose that a man is offered a promotion, which will entail moving to a different city, and suppose that he and his wife write down the reasons for and against accepting it. Reasons for accepting promotion include greater job-satisfaction, the stimulus of a new and bigger job, more money, and getting away from certain things in their present situation that they dislike; reasons against it include the leaving of friends, the disruption that might be caused in their children's education, and the strain of moving. As they consider the alternatives they believe that both are possible *and they are right*: contrary to what determinists say, it is genuinely possible for them to move, and it is also genuinely possible for them to stay where they are. At this point, then, if one were to say, 'They will move', one could be wrong, because it is possible for them to stay. That is, it is impossible to say with certainty what they are going to do.[7] The words 'with certainty' are important, for of course it is often possible to know what someone will *probably* do, and at times the probability can be so high as to be near-certainty, and one can act on one's estimate with almost complete confidence.

There are, then, three kinds of event in our universe: determined, random and free. Random and free events differ greatly from each other in that no one is responsible for what happens by chance, whereas persons are responsible for what they freely choose to do; but random and free events are alike in being undetermined and unpredictable. The existence of these events means that evolution has not followed a course that was predetermined in detail. Firstly, many things which exist today are the results of chance. For example, the chemical composition of the sea, the shapes of mountains and the range of electromagnetic radiation to which the human eye responds were probably not predetermined exactly, but happen by chance to be exactly what they are. Secondly, other things are the results of human free choices. For example, in the earliest stages of the universe, long before man existed, it was surely not already determined that we would now have our present alphabets or our number system based on ten: somewhere along the line human beings freely chose these. And, of course, national borders and many other things exist because of free choices made by leaders of nations and others. The course of evolution, then, was not predictable in detail, even in principle, and neither was, nor is the course of history entirely predictable.[8]

GOD'S RESPONSIBILITY
AND OUR OWN

There are some things which are theoretically, inherently or in principle possible, but which we today cannot make or do because we lack the knowledge or power. Other things, however, are inherently impossible: that we cannot make or do these implies no deficiency in us, and even God who is omnipotent cannot make or do them. Virtually everyone accepts this where logical impossibility is concerned (e.g., everyone agrees that God, though omnipotent, cannot draw a square circle); but if I am right in contending that there are other kinds of inherent impossibility besides the logical kind, then it is true of all kinds of inherent impossibility. And if it is true that a non-evolving material universe is inherently impossible, then it is wrong to suppose that while a painless world is inherently possible God was not strong enough to achieve it and the existing world is the rather poor best he could do; it is also wrong to suppose that God could have created a painless world but, instead, cruelly chose this one: the only possibilities were a world like ours and none at all. Hick says:

> His [God's] power is, by definition, not limited and not insufficient. It cannot be said that he *must* or that he *can only* create a world in which life devours life and in which creatures are wounded, maimed, starved, frozen, diseased, and hunted to their death.[1]

But Teilhard answers:

> *Not through inability*, but by reason of the *very structure of the nil* to which he stoops [I would rather say: because of the nature of

matter], God can proceed to creation *in only one way*: he must arrange, and, under his magnetic influence and using the tentative operation of enormous numbers, gradually unify an immense multitude of elements.[2]

The nature of matter is one reason. Human freedom is another. Take, for example, the cases of unmarried people who believe that they ought to be married, and of married people who believe that they made mistakes when they married their particular partners – and, let us make no mistake, these people may not be in physical pain but they are suffering. For such suffering not to occur, God would have to ensure the birth into each community of an exactly equal number of men and women desirous of marriage, such that they could all be matched in pairs with none left over; then, to make sure that no mistakes occurred, he would have to assign men and women to each other in pairs and *make* them marry each other: only thus could he ensure that there would be no unwilling bachelors or spinsters and no mismatched couples. God could not do that not because he is not omnipotent but because persons must be allowed to choose their partners for themselves.

On this supposition, let us put the question: 'Does God will the lack of order that is in the universe and the suffering it causes? Does God will the earthquakes and famines that occur, and did he will Keats' early death of tuberculosis?' To answer this with precision, it is necessary to distinguish between willing something directly, willing it indirectly, and merely not stopping it.

When one wills something saying to oneself simply and without qualification that one wills *it*, one is said to will it directly. If, for instance, a man wants a certain girl to marry him, or if he wants to win a game of tennis, then he wants *that*, and so can be said to will that directly. When, however, one wills something only in so far as it is inextricably linked with *something else*, then one is said to will it indirectly. We quite often will indirectly things which we would not will directly, but which are tied up, as unavoidable accompanying circumstances, with other things. For example, one wants to have a certain woman at one's party, but she will not come unless her obnoxious husband comes with her; one decides that it is worth while to put up with him for the sake of having her, and invites the two of them; they come, and there at one's party is the husband, being offensive, and there is no escaping the knowledge that one invited him: but one willed his presence indirectly, hers directly. Again, a surgeon performs an operation in the course of which he cuts through muscle though he knows that this will cause the patient a great deal of pain later. If he willed this pain directly, he would be a sadist; but, instead, he wills it only because of its connection with the good effect he wants to achieve – that is, he wills it indirectly. Merely not stopping is something else again. Suppose, for example, that a man's wife tells him that she is about to leave him and go to live with some other man; suppose that the husband believes that this decision by his wife will be disastrous in its consequences for himself, for their children and ultimately for her as well, but suppose that he sees that he has no chance of persuading her to change her mind. What is he to do? It might be physically possible for him to hold his wife in the house indefinitely as a prisoner, but it is wrong to assume total control of the life of a sane adult person against his or her will, and while we should help each other as far as we can and this includes saving each other from making mistakes, there is a point beyond which one may not go in endeavouring to help someone else, and when that point is reached one must draw back and let the other act, rightly disclaiming responsibility for what he or she does. The husband, then, sees that it would be wrong for him to lock his wife in as if she were a child that seemed determined to run away from home or as if she were not responsible for her actions; he sees that such an exercise of physical force would be an illicit interference with another person in the exercise of her free will; and so he does not physically intervene when she goes upstairs, packs a suitcase, carries it downstairs and out to her car, then gets in and drives away. Since it would have been physically possible for him to stop her, he may be said to have 'let her go' or to have 'not stopped' her departure, as the prodigal son's father let him leave home. From this example two differences between 'willing indirectly' and 'not stopping' emerge. First, one wills indirectly something bad that is linked with something good that one wants to get or do; but what one does not stop may have nothing good linked to it – or any good that it brings with it may not be important enough to outweigh its serious badness. Secondly, whereas one is responsible for what one indirectly wills, one is not as a rule responsible for what one does not stop someone else from doing – the other person is. Asked about something which one has indirectly willed, one assumes responsibility for it and justifies one's action by pointing to the good that was linked with it; but asked about something one did not stop another from doing, one replies by disavowing responsibility – if the husband in the story above were to be asked why he let his wife leave him, he would say, 'Because after I had said all I could say, she was still determined to go.'

If the terms are used in these senses, and if the theory I have called evolutionary optimism is right, then God does not will directly the unorder in the world and the troubles that afflict us of the kinds illustrated by the examples given earlier. On the other hand, he does more than merely not stop them. He wills them indirectly, because they are necessarily linked with the good he achieves by creating.

The next question is that of God's foreknowledge of the events that occur in the universe.

It is sometimes said that, being outside time, God is even now seeing future events happening. This means, it is said, that he knows all future events before they occur.

There is a fallacy here. An event is past, present or future in relation to a particular point in time. For instance, in the thirties World War II was the future war that some people were foreseeing; in the early forties it was the present war; now it is a past war. If God is outside time, he is not connected to any particular point of time, and therefore for him World War II is neither a past, present nor future war; he does not look back on events as past, and he does not look forward to events as future or 'know future events before they occur'. That is, the knowledge attributed to God in this view is not *fore*knowledge but simply knowledge; it is not *pro*vidence but simply 'vidence' or vision. The scholastic philosopher-theologians called it *scientia visionis*.

Moreover, the statement that 'God knows all future events' attributes to him knowledge that is, by hypothesis, useless. Knowledge of *some* future events can be useful: for instance, if a man learns that certain shares are going to rise he can buy some. But if one were to have true and certain knowledge of *all* future events, one would not be able to use it without adding events that had not been foreseen or preventing events that had been foreseen, and then the 'true and certain knowledge of all future events' and the events themselves would not match each other, which is a contradiction in terms. The scholastic philosophers who talked of *scientia visionis* knew this, and did not use it to explain God's control of events.

However, words and prefixes like 'then', 'prior', 'pre' and 'fore' can be used without implying intervals of time. If, for instance, we say, 'The angles of a triangle add up to two right angles; it follows then that the angles of an equilateral triangle are each of sixty degrees', we do not mean that the second statement became true some time after the first one: the word 'then' denotes logical, not temporal, sequence. And if we say, as I now do, that for God's decisions to be intelligent they must presuppose some knowledge, we do not mean that he obtains knowledge and some time afterwards makes decisions. We mean that his decisions are made in view of certain knowledge. We can then legitimately ask: What knowledge of event iss presupposed by God's decision to create? This is not an invitation to idle speculation. Far from it. We need to know the answer in order to know how God is involved in what happens to us.

If the question is admitted, then it comes to me, firstly, that God's decision to bring free beings into existence cannot presuppose knowledge of the decisions made by these beings, so that God does not, by either temporal or logical antecedence, *fore*see human free acts. It seems to me, secondly, that God decides to bring a material universe into existence, knowing that such a universe evolves and gives rise to rational beings who themselves evolve, but not foreknowing in detail all the events that occur in the course of the universe's development. Others besides me have made this assertion: indeed, William J. Hill OP says that 'contemporary serious thought is practically unanimous in denying to God an infallible knowledge of the future, precisely because there is as yet no such thing, either within the existing temporal order (obviously) or within what has traditionally been known as the eternity of God'.[3] One particular serious thinker who held this view was Maritain. He said that 'the impossibility of being foreseen with absolute certainty' is 'a property of the free act as such', and added: 'whatever comprehension or supercomprehension of causes one may have',[4] that is, even God cannot foresee free acts with certainty. He said:

> The divine plan is not a scenario prepared in advance, in which free subjects would play parts and act as performers. We must purge our thought of any idea of a play written in advance.

'On the contrary,' he said, 'everything is improvised.'[5] He drew the conclusion that in creation God takes risks and that free beings astonish God himself.[6]

But, it might be asked, what about God's omniscience? Just as God's omnipotence is his power to do whatever is inherently possible, so his omniscience is his knowledge of all that is inherently knowable: God, for instance, does not know the last digit of the square root of two expressed as a decimal because this is inherently unknowable. If, then, a free decision is inherently unknowable before it is made (taking 'before' in both temporal and logical senses), to say God does not know it prior to its actuality is not to attack his omniscience.

The fact must nevertheless be faced that in the Bible we find passages like this one, from a psalm:

> You had scrutinised my every action,
> all were recorded in your book,
> my days listed and determined,
> even before the first of them occurred.[7]

Wisdom, we read, 'knows the past, she forecasts the future'.[8] In Isaiah, Yahweh says:

> From the beginning I foretold the future,
> and predicted beforehand what is to be.[9]

> I revealed things beforehand,
> before they happened I announced them to you.[10]

In Daniel, we read that Susannah cried out: 'Eternal God, you know all secrets and everything before it happens' (Dan. 13.42). In the New Testament it is constantly said that events occur as had been foretold, and Jesus himself foretells his passion and death, not only in general but also giving details such as that he is going to be betrayed by Judas, handed over to the elders, chief priests and scribes and condemned to death by them, denied by Peter, handed over to the pagans, mocked, spit upon, scourged and finally crucified.

There seems to be in men a feeling that the future can be known, and people have consulted the stars, the insides of animals, crystal balls, Tarot cards, playing cards, tea-leaves, fortune-tellers, oracles and sooth-sayers in the endeavour to learn it. Thinking that it can be known, the Old Testament writers naturally believed that God knows it, and Isaiah contrasted Yahweh, who knows the future and reveals it accurately, with soothsayers, who get it wrong. In this as in other ways we must, I suggest, modify the idea they had of God's relationship with history. Where Jesus is concerned, let us begin by noting that no one can make a free choice knowing beforehand, with absolute certainty, what he is going to choose. (Imagine yourself saying: 'I haven't decided yet whether or not to read *The Lord of the Rings*. I'm still trying to make up my mind. Mind you, I know for a definite fact that I am going to decide to read it, but I haven't yet made the decision. It will probably take me another day or two.' This is psychologically and logically impossible, because it involves regarding an issue as both open and closed.) Therefore, if Jesus exercised free will during his life, he did not know all future events, and one cannot argue that because he knew all future events he knew beforehand all the details of his passion. The most reasonable course is to understand the passion prophecies not as reportage of events that he had seen by looking into the future, but as predictions based on his realization that the Jewish authorities had become resolutely hostile towards him. That is, they came from knowledge of the present, not the future, and they had the near-certainty that is not excluded by the unpredictability of free acts. As for the details, they were added later.

If what I have said about God's will and foreknowledge is true, then when a young person dies or a deformed child is born, and people ask, 'Did God want this to happen?', the best short answer is 'No – he didn't even know it was going to happen'. It can be added that when God decided to bring the world into existence he knew in general that things like that would happen in it, and he nevertheless went ahead and created the world; to that extent, he is responsible for these events. However, he did not will or even know particular events such as *this* death and *this* birth.

Our fundamental attitude towards the universe should surely be one of acceptance, for it is, on the whole, good. All is *not* right in it; not all its discord is harmony not understood; but we ought not to refuse to accept it because it is not perfect now. Rather, we should be like the owner of the field in the gospel parable who sees that he cannot pull out the darnel without destroying the wheat as well, but who does not destroy the whole field because of the darnel in it; instead, because of the wheat, he continues to accept the field and for the time being he tolerates the darnel. In the parable of the good and bad fish, the fishers realize that they are unable so long as they are at sea to separate the good from the bad, but they do not throw away the whole catch because there are bad fish in it; they tolerate the presence of the bad fish until they reach land and can separate them and throw them away. It is interesting to note that these parables are based on a kind of evolutionary view; the wheat and the darnel are growing and will be harvested, and the ships are on their way to land.

We must work. If total optimism implies that the universe is perfect as it is, so that nothing needs to be done to it, and that whatever we do will turn out to be for the best, so that there is no point in agonizing over our decisions; and if total pessimism implies that the universe is hopeless, so that there is ultimately no sense in trying to remedy its ills; the evolutionary world-view implies that there is a great deal to be done, that it is worthwhile to do it, and that is is our vocation to gather information, to make responsible decisions about what most needs to be done and how it can best be done, and then to *act* aggressively or gently to make the world a better place. The primary answer to the problem of the unorder and suffering in our world is, in this world-view, *action* or *work*. We can, and do, also ask God to act prayers of petition make sense in this system, as they do not in that of total optimism. The secondary attitude, I suggest, is dignified acceptance, which becomes right after all that could reasonably be done has been done.

5

CRITICISM OF EVOLUTIONARY OPTIMISM

Teilhard de Chardin believed that this theory solves the problem of evil in all its forms. He said in 1933:

> In this new [evolutionary] setting, while evil loses nothing of its poignancy or horror, it ceases to be an incomprehensible element in the structure of the world and becomes a *natural feature*.[1]

Towards the end of his life he was even more emphatic. In 1948 he wrote:

> Our ingrained habits of thought are such that we still automatically maintain that the problem of evil is insoluble. And yet, why should this be so? In the old cosmos, which was assumed to have emerged from the hands of the Creator, it was only natural to find it difficult to reconcile a partially evil world with the existence of a God who is both good and omnipotent. But with our modern view of a universe in a state of cosmogenesis [evolution] . . . how can so many well-ordered minds still persist in failing to see that, intellectually speaking, the only too familiar problem no longer exists?[2]

And in 1951 he wrote:

> When cosmogenesis is accepted, then . . . not only is there a solution to the problem of evil, but the problem itself *ceases to arise*.[3]

On the credit side, the theory does explain in a highly satisfactory way much of the unorder in the universe and much of the suffering we undergo and see. An opposing theory, of which

I shall have more to say later, attributes all the ills of the universe and all the lack of order in it to a moral fault on the part of some creature: it says that the universe would be in a state of perfection if it had not been partly spoiled by the consequences of moral evil. But the Lisbon earthquake, for example, was presumably caused by a cracking and slipping of the earth's crust as it cooled, and so its causal explanation reaches back to a time long before there were moral creatures on the earth. Again, the violence and rapacity that rage in the animal kingdom were there before the first men appeared, and are quite clearly part of the structure of our universe; and if animals at times attack and kill men, this seems in accord with nature as it now is and not a defect that was caused by someone's fault. Such ills, therefore, as the deaths of men in earthquakes or in attacks by wild animals resist the attempt to explain all ills as consequences of moral fault; but Teilhard's evolutionary theory explains them in an entirely reasonable way. It also explains some imperfections of the universe that are of the moral order, for by postulating that man's moral conscience evolves it explains how at one time men saw nothing immoral in slavery, how many societies have accepted polygamy, how some people even today are morally underdeveloped and cheat their fellowmen without compunction, and how others are unable to adapt to a society that is too highly developed for them, become uncontrollably resentful and involuntarily violent and destructive. It is also possible to explain why this theory has been formulated relatively recently, for until a short time ago the empirical evidence for evolution had not been found and recognized, and of course evolution provides the key to the problem.

On the debit side, however, stands, as I believe, the fact that this theory does not even begin to take account of knowing, deliberate, wicked, malicious wrongdoing and its physical consequences. In presenting it I have given examples of unorder, trouble and suffering and showed how they can be explained, but in none of the cases presented was anyone to blame for the unorder and the suffering. This was deliberate and necessary, because the theory does not work as an explanation of deliberate immoral acts and their consequences. I shall return to this point later, after analysing moral evil, but even at this stage it is surely evident that if a child dies because it contracts some disease that we are as yet unable to cure, or because it accidentally locks itself in a small space and there suffocates, we can perhaps reasonably tell the parents that human beings, especially children, are by nature fragile, that it is part of the human condition to be in fairly constant danger, and that it is inevitable that from time to time, in spite of every reasonable precaution being taken, a child will die by sickness or accident. We will redouble our efforts to find cures for diseases and to make the world a safer place for children to play in, but in the meantime such things will happen. However, if an unscrupulous manufacturer wickedly makes an appliance the safety of which he guarantees, though it is not safe and he knows it, and if a child's death is caused by this appliance, then one cannot speak to the parents in the same way: this incident could and should have been avoided, and is someone's fault, so that it is quite different. Neither can we say that just as there must be hundreds of musicians who fail to become great virtuosi for every one who succeeds, so there must be hundreds of criminals for every honest man, hundreds of adulterers for every faithful husband or wife, and so on: it is not the same.[4]

A certain blindness to moral evil characterized the proposers of evolutionary optimism in the latter part of the eighteenth century.[5] I think that a similar blindness to moral evil afflicted Teilhard de Chardin. He saw and experienced suffering: his sister had Pott's disease from 1903 until her death in 1936; he was a stretcher-bearer in the First World War; he was misunderstood, denounced, made to live in exile from Paris, not allowed to hold academic positions in the *Institut Catholique* or the *Collège de France*, and not permitted to publish his writings. But his sister's sickness was nobody's fault; he does not seem to have seen the war as a manifestation of sin at work in the world, or to have been aware of moral evil in the political and social sphere;[6] and the opposition he encountered in the church came from men who were ignorant, timid or prejudiced, but who were doing what they believed to be right. Also, as a geologist Teilhard saw evidence of physical unorder, waste and failure in the world, but of course none of moral evil. Many of his colleagues were atheists, and he thought that this was unfortunate, but he did not think that it was their fault and generally speaking he encountered in the scientific community only intellectual honesty disinterested dedication to research and co-operation between men of different nations. It need not, then, altogether surprise us if, while he was deeply aware of suffering, he failed to grasp the nature of moral evil. Almost all commentators on his work have made this criticism of him. I quote Tresmontant:

> There is, in human evil, a *remainder* which cannot be explained either in terms of the multiple nature nor yet by the temporality of the genesis in progress. The perversity of the concentration-camp butchers cannot be explained simply in terms of the Manifold! . . . Teilhard seems not to distinguish sufficiently between physical evil, which is susceptible of a natural explanation in terms of the unfinished state of creation, and the evil that springs from the sin of man.[7]

PART THREE

MORAL EVIL: ITS NATURE
AND CAUSE

6

MORAL EVIL

This and following chapters will be about moral evil and its physical consequences – that is, about precisely those things for which the Teilhardian theory does not account. First, however, it will be advisable to mention, in order to dismiss it from consideration, a kind of behaviour which has some appearance of moral evil but is not that: it is amoral behaviour.

Very young children have intelligence and use language, and in some degree they act with knowledge and deliberation, but their actions seem to be governed by their idea of what is to their practical advantage or disadvantage, and this is what the word 'ought' means to them, not a properly ethical obligation. If they behave well, then, their actions are not properly speaking moral or ethical, and if they behave badly their actions are not immoral: they are amoral beings.

Some adults – perhaps many – are amoral in certain areas of their lives. There exist criminals who have no sense of right or wrong where their criminal activities are concerned, but who have a strong sense of properly moral obligation where their families are concerned. That is, they do not feel any *moral* obligation to obey the law where their 'work' is concerned, and make all their decisions on the basis of the profit expected versus risk involved; but they feel a properly moral obligation to provide for their children's education and they comment on the bad moral character of other men who do not do this. I suspect that there also exist men who have a highly-developed ethical sense where their work is concerned, but who are amoral in their dealings with women. Moreover, moral obligation is sometimes explained by saying that when people say they 'ought' to do something they mean in the last analysis that it is to their practical advantage to do it. Guilt, then, is explained as a feeling of regret that people have on account of mistakes they have made about where their advantage lay; and it is said that the whole problem of guilt can be resolved simply by admitting one made a mistake, making a mental note not to make it again, and deciding not to cry over spilt milk. It seems to me that anyone who used 'ought' and 'guilt' only in these senses would be completely amoral and have had no experience of moral obligation and guilt but have found a way of using the words so that they meant something to him. As the theory is not rarely proposed, there probably are such people.

I propose to assume here, firstly, that properly moral obligations exist. I assume, for instance, that parents ought to take care of their children if they can and unless others are willing to do this for them; that members of juries ought to pay attention and make their decisions on the evidence put before them; that generally speaking people ought to keep their promises and pay their debts; and that the reason why people 'ought' to do these things is not because it is to their practical advantage but because a properly *moral* obligation exists to do them.

In assuming that man is a moral being I am, of course, again assuming that men have free will. The main implication of free will is not the unpredictability discussed earlier, but responsibility, for when nothing outside us or in us makes us do one thing rather than another, we freely choose and are responsible for our decisions, our actions, and their consequences so far as we foresee them. My second assumption is that God allows men to choose freely between morally good and morally bad alternatives, and to act accordingly. This is at least implicit in virtually all the Bible, for the commands, exhortations and reprimands from God suppose that men are free to act well or badly. It was the explicit teaching of many of the Greek Fathers of the church. Surrounded by people who believed that man's life is governed by fate or necessity, they did not reply: 'No, it is governed by God' but 'No, man governs himself.'[1]

Thirdly, I said earlier that God does not create knowing in advance what particular free beings will do,[2] and I shall assume here that this implies that he does not create knowing whether they will act morally or immorally.

I shall assume, fourthly, that the reason for a moral obligation is that some being has value. For example, if I see that someone is about to touch a wire which I know is at a high voltage I *must* call out 'Stop', because he has value. I do not say that I have an obligation because I attribute value to him; I have it because he has value and I recognize it.

Moral evil occurs when a person recognizes a moral obligation and deliberately acts against it.

They are purely interior immoral acts. One kind consists in deciding that one definitely would do something wrong if it were not for purely practical difficulties (for instance, it would cost too much money). Here one does not actually perform an outward immoral action, but one says yes in principle to such an action and decides to disregard morality and be governed by practical considerations only. This is wrong.

Wishes can be very wholehearted volitions, as is shown when someone wishes that a person he loves will recover from an illness; they can even be wholehearted when they cannot be fulfilled, as is shown when we wish that someone we love had not died, or when someone wishes that a person whom he or she loves had not married someone else; and another kind of immoral act consists in wishing something that one ought not to wish, and willing to go on wishing it. For instance, if one person really hates another and seriously wishes harm to come to him, the wish is immoral and the person is bad because of his wish even if he does nothing to bring about its fulfilment. A particular kind of morally wrong wish is wishing that someone else would do something immoral: it would, for instance, be immoral seriously to wish that someone would assassinate a world leader whom one happens to oppose.

Yet another kind of interior immoral act is being seriously glad about something that happened that it is wrong to be glad about. If, for instance, someone whom one dislikes is seriously hurt, it is wrong to rejoice in that; it is wrong to be glad about a wrong act committed in the past, whether by oneself or another person – it would, for instance, be wrong seriously to say: 'I believe it was morally wrong to drop the atomic bombs on Nagasaki and Hiroshima, but I am glad it was done, as it shortened the war.'

Secondly, there are outward actions, like the murder committed by Macbeth, who conceives the idea of hastening his predicted ascent to the throne by killing Duncan, who reflects on how unnatural and foul a deed that would be, but who makes up his mind to do it ('I am settled', he says) and does it.

Thirdly, a person can commit moral evil by deliberately not acting when he knows he should; and indecision can be immoral, too, for, as Buber says, at times 'intensification and confirmation of indecision is decision to evil'.[3]

It is sometimes possible to pinpoint the moment when a morally evil decision is made. However, this is not always possible. Perhaps, indeed, it is rarely possible. But obviously our inability to pinpoint a moment of decision should not lead us to conclude that there never was such a moment, or that no decision has been made. Moreover, if one person hates another, it hardly matters when precisely he chose to do so; if one person has the intention of doing something wrong, it does not very much matter when exactly he formed it: what matters about any person at any moment is what his freely held attitudes and intentions are at that moment.

For all its horribleness, moral evil is a real possibility. While we should not be quick in any particular case to declare that a morally evil act has been committed, we should not rule it out as impossible. It really can happen.[4] Perhaps each one of us is accompanied by a shadow which is the particular kind of bad person that he would probably become if he were to turn to evil – for one, a seducer, for another, a sadist – and which represents moral evil in the form in which it is most possible for him personally.

More than this, moral evil is a fact. Morally evil acts have been committed, as Vatican II said, 'from the very dawn of history', and in our times, as Menninger says, 'there *is* immorality; there *is* unethical behaviour; there *is* wrongdoing'.[5] Indeed, says Peter Berger of deeds committed in our time, certain deeds 'seem to violate a fundamental awareness of the constitution of our humanity'; they are 'not only evil, but *monstrously evil*'. It is, he says, impossible to say we think them evil because of the particular way we have been socialized; we are constrained to condemn them absolutely. 'Our condemnation is absolute and certain. It does not permit modification or doubt, and it is made in the conviction that it applies to all times and to all men as well as to the perpetrator or putative perpetrator of the particular deed.'[6] In the Nazi persecution of the Jews, for instance, after one had allowed for diminished responsibility or even some cases of no responsibility at all, there remains a residue that defies such explanation: that is moral evil.[7]

Certain decisions are serious, and others are of small moment. For instance, at one extreme are the choice of a career, the decision about whether or not to propose marriage or accept a proposal, and the decision about whether to become a priest or to cease to be one; at the other extreme are such decisions as whether or not to buy a newspaper. When making a serious decision we have to consider almost every area of our lives: for instance, a man wondering whether or not to propose to a certain woman thinks about his religion, his family, his friends, his work, his finances and his interests, because they all affect his decision or will be affected by it. But when making a small decision one does not do this – one's religion, family, friends and work are not involved in a decision about whether to order red wine or white. Also, by his serious decisions a man structures his life and makes himself the kind of man he is, whereas small day-to-day decisions do not affect our lives in any significant way. All this is a matter of observation, but it may also be remarked that life would be unbearable if at almost every moment we were obliged to make decisions involving and affecting our entire lives.

In the light of this we may distinguish between morally good acts which are important or serious, and others which are of little moment. If, for instance, someone intercedes for a victim of injustice, thereby endangering his own career and his standing in society, he performs a great morally good action, whereas if someone repays a debt of ten cents, he performs a morally good act of small moment. We may also distinguish between serious morally evil acts and morally bad acts of small moment. At one extreme are deep hatred of another person, injustice on a large scale and acts like Macbeth's; at the other extreme are knocking off work five minutes early, being impatient with an old man who cannot make up his mind quickly, or stopping to look at something in a shop window and thereby being late for an appointment. On the one hand, these lesser acts are bad, and one ought not to do such things. Also, they are signs of irresolution in one's intention to be a morally good person, and by such small acts a person can prepare himself for a seriously wrong action. But, on the other hand, they are not *serious* and by them a person does not introduce evil into the structure of his life or make himself a morally evil person. As Borhoeffer says, 'One sin, then, is not like another. They do not all have the same weight There are heavier sins and lighter sins.'[8] In all that follows I shall be considering only serious morally evil acts.

7

THE CONTENT OF THE MORALLY
EVIL ACT

Any decisions which one makes are concerned with objects which are expressly mentioned in one's interior monologue. 'I will fly to Paris', a man says to himself in London, and so decides quite expressly about Paris and an aeroplane. These decisions, however, as personal experiences, are also concerned with things which one knows about but does not expressly mention to oneself at the moments of making them. For instance, in deciding to fly to Paris he decides to spend some time in an enclosed space with some other people, to cross the Channel, to pay his fare and to do other things which, as he knows though he does not talk to himself about them, are included in flying to Paris. In deciding to post a cheque to pay a bill a person – usually without saying any of this over to himself – accepts, at least provisionally, private property, the monetary system, banks, the postal service and the government. Moreover, he accepts his own existence as a person, identified by his signature, and also the existence of other people and the world. There is, then, far more *in* our decisions than we express to ourselves when we make them, and indeed in every serious free act a man decides about his whole life. (Of course, to be the object of a decision as a personal experience, a thing must at least be known about by the person making the decision: if, for instance, I decide to drive a car which has a loose axle that I do not know about, the axle and the trouble it will cause are not *in* my decision.)

In this chapter I shall be concerned with the content of serious morally evil decisions. I shall be concerned not only with express or formulated intentions, but also with those which are more or less hidden and unexpressed, for these, too, are included in what the person wills and is responsible for. Here begins, then, a journey into darkness, as we explore the implications of a morally evil act and unravel the intentions which a person has when he decides to do something which he believes to be seriously wrong.

It might seem that in most morally evil acts people seek to do themselves good, at the expense of others and in spite of the moral law. Thinking along these lines, some writers say that moral evil springs from excessive self-love.[1] However, by hypothesis a person who commits a morally evil act does something which he believes is bad and so renders himself *in his own judgment* evil. Hence, as Paul Weiss says, wicked men oppose and defeat themselves;[2] or, as Simone de Beauvoir says, 'Evil is not at one with itself; self-laceration is its very essence'.[3] As Barth says, sin is 'at one and the same time a denial of God, a hatred of one's fellow and' – to come to what concerns us here – 'self-destruction'.[4] A sinner, as Bradley says of Macbeth, knowingly makes mortal war on his own soul;[5] in the extreme case he is 'dominated by the lust of self-demolition'.[6] Thomas Aquinas said that self-hatred is absolutely impossible,[7] but he was wrong. As Bernanos said, 'How easy it is to hate oneself!',[8] and there can be pleasure in it:

> He [Birkin] knew that his spirituality was concomitant of a process of depravity, a sort of pleasure in self-destruction. There really *was* a certain stimulant in self-destruction, for him – especially when it was translated spiritually.[9]

Fromm shrewdly observes: 'The selfish person does not love himself too much but too little: in fact he hates himself',[10] and this self-hate is in all forms of moral evil.

Also, morally evil acts often contain hatred of others and the will to hurt or even annihilate them. Lady Chatterley experienced this in her adultery:

> She realized for the first time what a queer subtle thing hate is. For the first time, she had consciously and definitely hated Clifford [her husband], with vivid hate: as if he ought to be obliterated from the face of the earth. And it was strange, how free

and full of life it made her feel, to hate him and to admit it fully to herself.[11]

The will to destroy another person is quite explicit in Valmont's peculiarly heartless seduction of the virtuous lady in *Les liaisons dangereuses*. He wants to possess her, but he declares, firstly, that he wants her to continue to believe in God and in virtue and to be terrified of sin and damnation:

> Far be it from me to destroy the prejudices which sway her mind! They will add to my happiness and my triumph. Let her believe in virtue, and sacrifice it to me; let the idea of falling terrify her, without preventing her fall; and may she, shaken by a thousand terrors, forget them, vanquish them only in my arms. Then, I agree, let her say to me: 'I adore thee' . . . I shall be truly the God whom she has preferred.[12]

He wants her, he says, 'to let her virtue expire in a slow agony'.[13] Secondly, he has made up his mind that at the end he will not ask her to become his mistress, but will woo her until she asks him, thereby making her fall from virtue all the greater.[14] Thirdly, he intends subsequently to reject her, and to let the world know that he has had an affair with her and then rejected her; this will hurt her feelings, ruin her reputation and publicly humiliate her. The intention of hurting another person is rarely as openly acknowledged as in these cases, but it is present, nevertheless, in many immoral actions.

Any genuine human community is held together by respect for persons and by the common acceptance of certain values. Often by evil actions men break away from groups to which they have belonged, or they offend a group and disgrace it: in some cases they cease to belong to groups of which they were previously members, and in other cases they remain members but are estranged from the other members. Thus a person who commits serious moral evil opts for outsiderhood or alienation from his fellow human beings. This is extremely clear in Sade, whose system 'is based upon the primary fact of absolute solitude',[15] achieved by total negation of others: 'For the Unique Person, all men are equal in their nothingness, and the Unique One, by reducing them to nothing, simply clarifies and demonstrates this nothingness.'[16] Byron expresses it, too, when his hero sets out

> to separate
> Himself from all who shared his mortal state.[17]

For such a one, 'hell is alone'[18] or 'hell is other people'[19] – other people are absent, or if present are enemies – and he has chosen hell. One might think that in sexual sins persons are united, but in Camus's *The Fall* Clamence says. 'True debauchery is liberating because it creates no obligations. In it you possess only yourself.'[20] And Saint-Exupéry's sage says.

> I . . . got nothing of my sensual pleasure but the morose and futile satisfaction of a miser's greed. Seeking, I found but myself.[21]

Moral evil often involves the wilful doing of damage to human institutions, structures, systems and codes of behaviour. It is one thing for a person to believe that some human institution is bad and endeavour to destroy it; of that I am not talking here, since it is not immoral. It is quite another thing for someone to understand, perhaps without having thought the matter out, that some institution – private ownership and the rules which have been worked out to protect and limit it, marriage and the code of sexual ethics, or the state – is an important human achievement which men have taken centuries to develop to its present state, and which is necessary for the physical, intellectual and moral well-being of people, and for him then to harm it; and much moral evil involves doing this. Someone who is dishonest, for example, sees that we have evolved a system to facilitate the exchange of goods and services, and he damages it, if only by undermining the trust between people that is necessary for it to work smoothly. Similarly, someone who deliberately disobeys a legitimate authority, knowing he is in the wrong, undermines that authority and implicitly wills the destruction of the system to which it is essential. Again, through centuries of experience human beings have come to see what respect for persons demands of us in the context of sexual relationships and behaviour, and so to agree on certain moral laws governing sexual behaviour; if someone is sexually immoral, he undermines the acceptance of these laws, with which, by hypothesis, he himself agrees; and so he takes us backwards towards the lawlessness and unhappiness that we are trying to leave further and further behind.[22] More generally, a sinner wants to 'cancel and tear to pieces that great bond'[23] which is the moral law, and bring into being a world where rights are disregarded and moral anarchy prevails. Moreover, a sinner denies reason: he calls evil good, good evil, he puts darkness for light and light for darkness (Isa. 5.20), and he deliberately becomes absurd in his thinking (see Rom. 1.21). In his own mind, and wherever his influence reaches, he destroys good sense.

Acceptance is an act of the will in which a person is not creative, but gives assent to what he finds already in existence; and a good person accepts reality. I do not mean that he accepts everything that exists, just as it is, any more than we mean, when we say that someone loves a city, that he loves everything in it. I mean that he sees that a world is *there* and is not his own mental construction or real creation, and he accepts it in general; he willingly accepts the fact that other persons exist besides himself and that they have value in themselves; he accepts himself; and he recognizes certain values which are in some sense outside him. This acceptance might seem at first to be servile acquiescence rooted in powerlessness, but the good person accepts reality (including the fact that other persons exist) generously, because he sees it as good, not submissively, because while he would like to change it he cannot. He may – indeed, he should – refuse to accept some particular real beings, but this does not cancel his acceptance of reality; indeed, his refusal derives from his more basic acceptance.[24] The acceptance of reality may never be expressed, but is present in every serious good act.[25] Now when a person refuses to respect the value of other persons, or refuses some elements of human institutions that are not merely conventional but (as he himself believes) necessary, or when he refuses to act in accord with his own essential nature, he implicitly says no to reality: acting as a subject, he sets himself against objective reality as such. He says no to being.

This no is not a simple turning of the mind away from reality, choosing to ignore it but wishing it no harm. On the contrary, whoever performs an immoral act takes a positively hostile attitude towards reality: he wills it away; he wills the void. Macbeth does not simply decide to ignore the moral order, but wills it to be torn to pieces, and Iago is dedicated to the destruction of what is good and healthy – he would, if he could, wipe out being. Milton's Satan destroys,

> For only in destroying I find ease
> To my relentless thoughts.[26]

Goethe's Mephistopheles says.

> I am the Spirit that always denies!
> And rightly so, for everything that comes into being
> Deserves to be destroyed.[27]

And one of Sade's characters says.

> Oh, what a pleasure it is to destroy! . . . I know of nothing more deliciously enjoyable. There is no ecstasy like that which one enjoys when one gives oneself up to this divinely infamous action.[28]

All of Sade's writing, indeed, is expressive of a will to destroy which reaches not only other people but Nature or being itself.

> It is she [Nature] I should like to outrage. I should like to upset her plans, thwart her progress, arrest the wheeling courses of the stars, throw the spheres floating in space into nightly confusion, destroy what serves Nature and protect what is harmful to her: in a word, insult her in her works.[29]

In Claudel's *Partage de midi* Mesa says, 'There is no tomorrow' and his mistress Ysé replies.

> You are right, there is no tomorrow . . . .
> There is no more past. no more future, no more husband, no children, no, no, no. There is nothing. *Nada*. Nothing at all. . . .
> Our desire is not to create but to destroy.
> Let there be nothing in existence but you and me, and in you only me, and in me only your possession and rage and tenderness and the desire to destroy you. . . .
> Ah, it is not your happiness I bring you, but your death and mine with it.[30]

This is what Barth has in mind when he says that moral evil involves *das Nichtige*, or the will for the void, and F. A. Staudenmaier says that sin negates being, truth, order and law, but is not satisfied with mere negation – 'it wants to *liquidate*, to *annihilate*, to *destroy*, what it negates'.[31] This manifested itself in Nazism: as Simon says, 'The victims of Auschwitz died because pagan madness wished to extirpate the light and to rule the world in dark, ecstatic nihilism.'[32] It was undoubtedly with Nazism in mind that Bonhoeffer wrote.

> The void towards which the west is drifting is not the natural end, the dying away and decline of a once flourishing history of nations. It is . . . a rebellious and outrageous void, and one which is the enemy of both God and man. . . . It is the supreme manifestation of all the powers which are opposed to God. It is the void made god. No one knows its goal or its measure. Its dominion is absolute. It is a creative void, which blows its anti-god's breath into the nostrils of all that is established and awakes it to a false semblance of new life while sucking out from it its proper essence, until at last it falls in ruin as a lifeless husk and is cast away. The void engulfs life, history, family, nation, language, faith. The list can be prolonged indefinitely, for the void spares nothing.[33]

Finally, after literary men and theologians I quote a psychologist, Erich Fromm, who says that men are at times malignantly aggressive, cruel and destructive not in order to achieve useful purposes but for the sheer lustful pleasure of destroying. He talks of 'that form of aggression which is characteristic of man and which he does not share with other mammals: his propensity to kill and to torture without any "reason", but as a goal in itself, a goal not pursued for the sake of defending life, but as desirable and pleasureful in itself',[34] and of 'the wish to destroy for the sake of destruction'.[35]

We have now reached what is in every serious immoral act: the will to evil. Sometimes the good is defined as that which is willed, or the will is defined as the faculty whose object is the good, and then it is said that a will to evil is a contradiction in terms and hence impossible. But definitions should be based on experience, and the will should be defined as the faculty of striving towards or withdrawing from, accepting or rejecting, desiring or abhorring, and choosing between, objects that are known and actions that are thought of; and the good should be defined as that which has what its nature requires it to have, or that which suits some other being's nature. A will to evil is not excluded by these definitions.

Many authors shy away from the idea that man can will what he knows to be evil. Mercier said: 'Evil as such is never willed',[36] and William Temple said: 'That any man ever chose evil, knowing it to be evil *for him*, is to me quite incredible.'[37] It seems to me that these authors have failed to see how dark a place the human heart can be. Biblical authors saw it; they saw that man can 'love evil more than good, and lying more than speaking the truth' (Ps. 52.3); they knew he can 'love all words that devour' (Ps. 52.4) and 'have pleasure in unrighteousness' (II Thess. 2.12); they knew about 'the fascination of wickedness' (Wisd. 4.12) and about men who have a fierce will to evil; and when they exhort us to 'seek good, and not evil' (Amos 5.15), to 'hate evil, and love good' (Amos 5.15) and 'hate what is evil, hold fast to what is good' (Rom. 12.9), they know the opposite to be possible. Some of the Greeks, also, had an idea of it. Ricoeur remarks that for them hubris was 'something like a deliberate will, distinct from being led astray by desire and from being carried away by anger – an intelligent will to evil for the sake of evil'.[38] Shakespeare, too, clearly believed that man can will what he knows to be evil. Macbeth is fully conscious of the fact that what he is doing is evil.

> Let not light see my black and deep desires,[39]

he says, but he himself sees them and how black they are – in his 'If it were done when 'tis done' speech he goes over in his mind the reasons why the deed he is going to commit is evil. Lady Macbeth expresses a fierce will to be unwomanly, inhuman unnatural, cruel, and in a word evil – she wants, she says, to be filled with direst cruelty, she wants nothing to shake her fell purpose, she wants murdering ministers, nature's mischief and thick night,[40] all of which clearly means that she fully intends to do evil. In *Titus Andronicus*, Aaron's only regret is that he has not done more evil in his life:

> Even now I curse the day – and yet, I think,
> Few come within the compass of my curse –

> Wherein I did not some notorious ill,
> As kill a man, or else devise his death,
> Ravish a maid, or plot the way to do it,
> Accuse some innocent and forswear myself,
> Set deadly enmity between two friends,[41]

and so on for another ten lines. As Helen Gardner says, there is in Shakespeare's plays pure spiritual malevolence, absolute or sheer ill-will, 'implacable malevolence, a hardness of heart that appals' and that cannot be reduced to anything comprehensible.[42] Milton's Satan could hardly be more explicit. 'Evil, be thou my good', he says.[43] Sade's character, Madame de Clairwil, requires of Juliette that she cease doing evil things in order to obtain sexual pleasure, and begin to do them in order to do evil. Dostoyevsky, too, saw the possibility of the will to evil, and the strange attraction that the idea of doing evil can have. Dmitry Karamazov says. 'I loved vice and I loved the feeling of shame that vice gave me. I loved cruelty.'[44] And Lise Khokhkakov says. 'I simply don't want to do good. I want to do evil.'[45] In one of Edgar Allan Poe's stories the narrator says.

> And then came, as if to my final and irrevocable overthrow, the spirit of PERVERSENESS. Of this spirit, philosophy takes no account. Yet I am not more sure that my soul lives, than I am that perverseness is one of the primitive impulses of the human heart – one of the indivisible primary faculties, or sentiments, which give direction to the character of man. Who has not, a hundred times, found himself committing a vile or a silly action, for no other reason than because he knows he should *not*? Have we not a perpetual inclination, in the teeth of our best judgement, to violate that which is *Law*, merely because we understand it to be such? This spirit of perverseness, I say, came to my final overthrow. It was this unfathomable longing of the soul to *vex itself* – to offer violence to its own nature – to do wrong for the wrong's sake only – that urged me to continue.[46]

Lautréamont's creation Maldoror 'sinks down into the vertiginous abysses of evil' and says: 'When I commit a crime I know what I am doing. I would not wish to do otherwise!'[47] So much for the cheerful thought that no one ever intends evil, itself.[48] When a person believes in God, his evil will has a religious character, and his acts are sins (I take immorality to be an ethical concept, but sin to be a religious one). In so far as he says no to being and knows that God is the ground of being, he says no to God. He wishes God were not there, or that he himself were God. As Heim says, 'if we are God's enemies then we want to dethrone God. . . . We wish God were not there.'[49] Barth says that in sin 'man does want to pass his limits, to be as God'; it is a vain wish, of course, but 'the impotence of the enterprise does not alter the fact that for all its perversion it does take place';[50] 'pride is a very feeble word to describe this. The correct word is perhaps megalomania'.[51] Moreover, the sinner hates God, like the men of whom Jesus said. 'They have seen and hated both me and my Father' (John 15.24). In certain evil cults this comes into the open, and in Sade's writings it is expressed frequently and violently, for Sade was obsessed by God and on page after page he shows his hatred for him. Also, in so far as the sinner wills the destruction of being, his will is to destroy God. As Heim says, rebellion against God 'assumes superhuman proportions and a demoniacal character and aims at the destruction of God.'[52] As Vergote says. 'Christ makes sin say what at first it did not quite say: that in the end it is murder of the Father'; Christ manifested sin 'by letting evil accomplish, on his person, the murder [of God] that it signified already in the half-dark of impulsive desires'.[53]

THE MYSTERY OF EVIL

In Chapter 3 I maintained that a reason why the world is not in perfect order is that it has not completed its growth: for instance, people are killed in earthquakes because we have not yet learned how to predict them accurately. The presence of moral evil in the world, however, cannot be explained in this way,[1] because it cannot be understood as mere lack of perfection.[1] Deliberate murderous violence is not mere lack of gentleness, gross selfishness is more than a lack of consideration for others, hatred is not lack of love (to be hated means far more than not to be loved, even by someone by whom one should be loved) and pride is not a name we have for an absence, a nothingness, that exists when a man has no humility. In general, a vice is not the mere absence of the corresponding virtue, but a driving force; it is not merely non-constructive, but positively destructive; it is not the non-assertion of some value or the non-willing of some good, but 'active positive negation'[2] and the willing of evil. If it is symbolized by darkness, this is not the darkness that most of us want to have when we switch off the light to go to sleep, or the darkness that comes over a peaceful countryside when the sun goes down and the stars come out; it is horrible darkness that one might find in a fairy-tale or remember from one's childhood – no mere absence of light but an almost tangible reality charged with menace and about to devour us. If a man goes into a remote jungle, meets natives who see him as an invader and kill him, we can say that his death was due to the natives' primitiveness and that if all men could be educated such deaths would cease. If, however, an educated man, who knows exactly what he is doing and that it is wrong, deliberately, cruelly and for selfish reasons reduces some other people to poverty, the case is totally different. And, as Hick says, taking a more extreme case, 'to describe, for example, the dynamic malevolence behind the Nazi attempt to exterminate the European Jews as merely the absence of some good, is utterly insufficient'. He goes on. 'The evil will as an experienced and experiencing reality is not negative. It can be a terrifyingly positive force in the world.'[3] And as Ricoeur says, 'Evil is not nothing; it is not a simple lack, a simple absence of order; it is the power of darkness; it is posited.'[4]

A person commits a morally evil act when he has before him two or more alternatives, one of which he believes to be wrong for him here and now, and he deliberately opts for it. Nothing antecedent to the choice itself, whether outside or inside himself – not his nature, the circumstances, nor the objects under consideration – and nothing outside himself acting at the moment of choice makes him choose as he does, and hence nothing outside his own self at the moment of choosing provides a causal explanation of the choice: one can only say, of this as of any other free choice, that the person chooses as he does because he so decides, and hence he is responsible for his choice. God leaves us free to make our own decisions, says Sirach; if, then, you do anything wrong,

> Do not say, 'The Lord is responsible for my sinning',
>   for he is never the cause of what he hates.
> Do not say, 'It was he who led me astray',[5]

but – the writer clearly implies – face the fact that you did wrong because you chose to do so. The Greek Fathers, who said that God made men free and independent, said that if a man sins it is because he chooses to do so. For instance, John Chrysostom said in effect that the entire explanation of Judas's betrayal of Christ is in Judas himself: he did that because he chose to do it.[6] Augustine said. 'Nothing else can make the mind the companion of evil desire except its own will and free choice';[7] 'we do evil from the free choice of the will';[8] and 'the movement by which the soul turns away from God towards the creature is its own movement'.[9] He went on to say that when we say a man does evil because he chooses to do so we have arrived at the root of evil, or have given the ultimate explanation. 'A perverse will,' he said, 'is the cause of all evil. . . . But if you are looking for the cause of this root, how will it be the root of all evil?'[10] 'The will itself is ultimately the cause of sin';[11] 'sin must be imputed to the will alone and we need look no further for the cause of sin.'[12] Kant insisted on the same point. Speaking of moral evil, he said. 'Man himself is its author';[13] ' "moral evil" is possible only as a determination of the free will';[14] 'man *himself* must make or have made himself into whatever, in a moral sense, whether good or evil, he is or is to become. Either condition must be an effect of his free choice (*Willkur*); for otherwise he could not be held responsible for it and could therefore be *morally* neither good nor evil.'[15]

In many free decisions it is evident that the person who makes them fixes in himself an abiding personal intention. The person, for example, who decides to be a doctor gives a 'set' to his will, which he actively keeps for the rest of his life, and two people deciding to marry make similar decisions. Many morally evil decisions are of this kind, for they are concerned not with simple acts but with the whole future life of the person concerned: for instance, a person who steals something generally means to keep it, and a person who enters into an adulterous relationship intending it to be permanent commits himself to a life of moral evil extending into the future as far as he can see, and as time goes on he keeps this intention and indeed strengthens it. In other free decisions it might at first appear that only a single act is involved and that once it has been performed no abiding intention remains in the will. It might appear, for instance, that if a man decides to take an afternoon off, with no intention of making this a regular practice, and does so, then next day it is all over and nothing remains. It might also appear that if a man were to decide to commit adultery once, and once only, and do so, then afterwards he would have no abiding evil intention. However, when a person makes up his mind to do something and does it, there normally remains in him *the will to have done it*, and this is an abiding intention differing from those mentioned above only by being concerned with a past act rather than with an ongoing series of acts. Suppose, for instance, that a man comes upon the scene of a car accident and springs into action, giving first aid, calling for an ambulance and looking after the victims while waiting for the ambulance to come. It is probable

that for the rest of his life he will remember his actions and
re-will them by willing to have done them (the opposite would
be for him to wish later that he had not done them). If then, a
person decides to do some single morally wrong thing, there
normally remains in him, as an abiding intention, the will to
have done it, and this intention is evil.

The moral quality of a person at any moment is determined
by his intentions at that moment. If he is continually doing
good and has no intention of doing any wrong, and if he has no
will to have done anything evil in the past, then he is a morally
good person. If he has been doing wrong and intends to go on
doing it, if he has the intention of doing something evil in the
future, or if he has done wrong at some time in the past and
now wills to have done it, then he is morally bad, or guilty.[16]

One of the most puzzling of questions is: how is it psychologically possible for human beings to do wrong?

Some say that in the last analysis all moral evil is due to ignorance or error. There is no doubt that many people do things
which are wrong, but which they mistakenly think are all right;
however, if a person does not believe that what he is doing is
wrong, it is not an immoral act, so that what we have here is not
an explanation of how moral evil occurs but the assertion that
there is no such thing.

In several places[17] Maritain has expounded what he says is
Thomas Aquinas's explanation of how people make morally
wrong decisions. If, he says, we consider what a person is
thinking about immediately before making a bad decision, we
find that he is not thinking about the rule which he is about to
break. This not-thinking is nothing positive; it is a mere absence
of thought. It is voluntary and free, but it is not in itself culpable
because we are not obliged to be thinking of all moral rules all
the time and because it is a mere absence. It is the root of sin,
but it is not itself a sin. If, then, we ask how a man can come to
do something morally wrong, we have here an explanation:
immediately beforehand he was not thinking of the moral rule
he was about to break. Maritain says that it is a fundamental
thesis of St Thomas that 'the *cause* of moral evil or of sin is a
failure of the will, to wit, the voluntary and free non-considera-
tion of the rule, which is not yet culpable, because it is a mere

negation, not a privation'.[18] There may be more in this than meets the eye, but it looks like an effort to make moral evil fit the definition of evil as 'privation', and to avoid facing the fact that in moral evil a person opts for evil. The difficulties with it are, firstly, that as a matter of fact some people do think about the moral law at the very moment of deciding to break it. Other people decide to do something immoral and then subsequently say to themselves that what they have decided to do is wrong, but that they will nevertheless do it, so that there is a moment when the immoral decision and the moral law are together at the front of their minds. Secondly, according to Maritain a person voluntarily does not think about the law he is on the point of breaking. Now no one is obliged to think of all moral laws all the time, but a person is obliged to think of any moral laws that concern a serious act he is thinking of performing, since deliberately not to do so amounts to a rejection of morality, and therefore this voluntary not-thinking about the relevant moral law is a culpable inaction (though Maritain says it is not culpable), and we are no nearer an explanation of how it is psychologically possible for a person to commit moral evil. Thirdly, what one habitually knows enters into one's act even if one does not expressly think about it at the moment of decision.

Some authors explain bad actions by saying that the sinner has a flawed nature, for which he himself is not responsible. Hick, for instance, says that

> the idea of an unqualifiedly good creature committing sin is self-contradictory and unintelligible. If the angels are finitely perfect, then even though they are in some important sense free to sin they will never in fact do so. If they do so we can only infer that they were not flawless.[19]

He insists that 'to say that an unqualifiedly good (though finite) being gratuitously sins is to say that he was not unqualifiedly good in the first place',[20] and says that the idea that God made angels and men free

> and that they themselves inexplicably and inexcusably rebelled against him . . . amounts to a sheer self-contradiction. It is impossible to conceive of wholly good beings in a wholly good

world becoming sinful. To say that they do is to postulate the self-creation of evil *ex nihilo*! There must have been some moral flaw in the creature or in his situation. [21]

Clearly, Hick is not saying that *sometimes* people do evil because of flaws in their natures; he is saying that without such a flaw sin is utterly impossible, or that *any* wrong act can be explained as the result of an antecedent disposition. Anatomize Regan, he says in effect, and you find she is naturally hard-hearted; that is why she is cruel; Macbeth is over-ambitious *and therefore* murders Duncan; and any evil deed that has ever been committed can be similarly explained. Erich Fromm maintains that it is not true that all human beings have an innate tendency to be malignantly aggressive; however, he maintains that if the social conditions in which people live make it impossible for them to develop properly, they acquire destructive characters *and therefore* they act destructively. [22] Quite the opposite view was expressed by various Fathers of the church. Cyril of Jerusalem, for instance, said: 'There is not one class of souls [persons] who sin by nature, another who are just by nature; all souls do good or evil by their free-will; they all have the same nature.' [23] Irenaeus said.

> If it was by nature that some are bad and others good, the latter would not be praiseworthy by virtue of being good, since they would have been created such, and the former would not be blameworthy, because they would have been made such. But in fact all are of the same nature, capable of holding and doing good, capable also of refusing it and not doing it. [24]

There is overstatement here: some people have tendencies or antecedent dispositions which amount to flaws in their natures, so that not all of us have quite the same natures. However, as Kant remarked, in principle a person who has no bad tendencies can commit moral evil; [25] and Hick must face the dilemma: if a person with a tendency to violence (for example) is provoked, is it possible for him to restrain himself? If not, his violent behaviour is perfectly explained by his natural tendency, but it is not morally evil and hence it is irrelevant to the present discussion. If, on the other hand, he can restrain himself, but becomes violent, his behaviour is morally evil but the question arises:

'Why did he give free rein to his violent tendency though he knew it was wrong to do so?' and merely to say that he has a tendency to violence does not answer this question.

Sometimes morally evil acts are explained by saying that they are committed under the evil influence of some other person who is immoral: Adam commits sin under the influence of Eve, who has already committed it; in the middle ages it was thought that if a man committed fornication he did so because of the influence of a particular devil, the spirit of fornication; and Macbeth commits murder under the influence of his wife. Clearly, there are two difficulties involved in this as an ultimate explanation. First, for the act to be immoral the person must be capable of withstanding the influence of his tempter; therefore, if he yields to influence and commits sin, the question arises, 'Why did he yield to the other person's influence even though he knew it was wrong and harmful to do so?' That is, the essence of the morally evil act – the person's choice of moral evil on his own responsibility – is not explained by pointing to an outside influence. This is clear in the case of Adam, and also in that of Macbeth, who never suggests that either his wife or the witches caused him to act as he did. Secondly, the question arises: 'This other person – how is his or her moral evil to be explained?' The tendency has been to reach back beyond the tempter to yet another person: thus Eve was influenced by the serpent, the spirit of fornication was thought to be driven by Lucifer, and the witches in Macbeth seem to have evil spirits as their masters and in particular to be subject to Hecate. One cannot go on like this indefinitely, and therefore there must be a being who commits moral evil without being influenced by another person to do so.

Others have said that moral evil is the choosing of one good rather than another: the lesser good rather than the greater; lesser benefits now rather than greater benefits later; sensual satisfaction rather than spiritual satisfaction like the peace of a good conscience; or one's own good rather than the general good.[26] They say that what makes sin psychologically possible is the ability we have to concentrate our attention on the first member of any of these pairs, and the good that is in it. But in an immoral act a person chooses not a lesser good but an evil, and not his private good but his own destruction.

Some writers define sin as turning away from God towards the creature, which seems psychologically understandable. If commitment to God were irreconcilable with commitments to other people or to human causes, this statement would make sense: the good person would then be turned away from creatures, towards God, and the bad person would have taken exactly the opposite direction. However, the good person is turned towards God and also towards creatures; and moral evil is a turning away from God and also a turning away from – or even a will to destroy – creatures. As Schoonenberg says, sin is a No to God, but also a No to one's fellow men, indeed to the whole creation, so that 'when sin is defined as "a turning away from God towards the creature" (*aversio a Deo, conversio ad creaturam*), that formula . . . is, by itself, incorrect, and a source of harmful misunderstandings'.[27] It therefore remains a mystery how it is psychologically possible for people to commit morally evil acts.

Another puzzle is: how can moral evil have a place in human life and in the scheme of things that is our universe?

It has been suggested that it has a place in human life because it does men and women good to have actual experience of moral evil: it opens their eyes to the dark side of reality, of which they might otherwise be unaware; it makes them feel their need for forgiveness; it cures them of any inclination they might have to arrogance; and it makes them understanding and sympathetic towards others who commit sins. However, the normal effect of sin is not to make a person aware of moral evil so much as to dull that awareness – as Monden says, 'every sin makes us blind to that awareness of sin'. Also, for every person who commits a moral fault, repents like Peter and is perhaps the better for the whole experience, there are others who after their moral falls despair and never recover their moral goodness, who commit suicide like Judas, or who tell themselves (without really believing it) that what they have done is perfectly all right and go on in bad faith to do it again. Moreover, it is by no means certain that committing sins makes a person sympathetic towards sinners: Christ, who was sinless, was very sympathetic, whereas reformed sinners can be harsh. Finally, no one who has even half understood the terrific evil force of sin could suggest that a dose of it might do anyone good.

The explanation of evil offered by total optimism, according to which every sin has good rather than bad effects in the long run, has already been dealt with. It has also been shown that moral evil does not 'fit into' Teilhard's evolutionary world-view or find its explanation there: whether in individual persons or in the human race as a whole, moral evil is not, like ignorance, a deficiency which is remedied by growth and effort; rather, the more persons develop, the greater becomes their capacity for moral evil. Also, whereas some suffering may be the price of progress, moral evil tends to destroy whatever progress has been made.

Another conceivable explanation of moral evil is that it is statistically necessary. In a present-day city of several million people there will in the course of a year occur some cases of cheating, theft, adultery, perjury and dangerous driving which will be morally evil acts; this implies that it is in some way necessary that such cases occur, though of course no particular case can involve necessity. However, people today are living in a world that has been shaped by moral evil committed in the past, so that if moral evil must occur today it is at least in large measure because it has been occurring. Therefore, to explain moral evil as statistically necessary *in the world of today* is to explain some moral evil by other moral evil, and hence not to explain why moral evil exists at all. What we have to consider, therefore, is whether moral evil is statistically necessary in the first place, or to put it the other way round, whether it would be inherently impossible, with a statistical impossibility, for a multitude of human beings to exist without some of them committing moral evil sometimes. Joseph Rickaby said:

> If it be asked how there can be a necessity of sin occurring which is not a necessity in any individual, let it be observed that where there is a real trial of free will there is real likelihood of sin: but a multitude of such likelihoods mean a necessity of sin somewhere.[28]

Maritain said: 'If it is in the nature of things that an event can happen, this event actually will happen sometimes';[29] human beings can do wrong, he said, and therefore they sometimes do so. Sertillanges said that the fact that glass is fragile means that inevitably some glass is broken; similarly, he said, the fact that human beings are morally fragile means that inevitably some commit sin. Teilhard said that in a system which is in process of organization it is *statistically* inevitable that disorders appear, and that this implies that in an evolving universe with human beings in it it is statistically inevitable that sins be committed.[30]

Statistical necessity is sometimes clearly grounded in the nature or basic structure of the universe: for instance, approximately equal numbers of male and female human beings are needed, and so it is natural that the probability of any particular baby being a boy or girl is approximately 50 per cent; also, though this is less evident, the process of evolution necessarily involves the production of some beings with congenital defects,[31] and so it is demanded by the structure of the universe that a probability exists that a particular child will prove to be congenitally deficient. But moral evil is anti-natural and destructive of the universe; it could not, then, be statistically necessary with a necessity grounded in the nature of things. Also, the universe as it comes from God, prior to the free choice of any creature, could not have within it, as an essential element, a hatred of God and the will to destroy him; but this would be the case if moral evil were statistically necessary. Surely, then, moral evil cannot be statistically necessary in the universe as such, and C. S. Lewis is right when he says. 'I think the most significant way of stating the real freedom of man is to say that if there are other rational species than man, existing in some other part of the actual universe, then it is not necessary to suppose that they also have fallen.'[32]

The fact is that it is no use trying to explain moral evil or to justify its existence. It is inexcusable, unjustifiable and inexplicable. Shakespeare saw this. Some of his characters have 'monstrous and inexplicable wickedness', which 'cannot be reduced or explained. . . . It terrifies because it is inexplicable'.[33] In his two-volume study of sin first published around 1840, Julius Müller said that moral evil is 'in its nature inconceivable, i.e., incomprehensible', and that it is 'the inscrutable mystery of the world; it ever remains, in its inmost depth, impenetrable darkness. This inconceivableness holds true of *every sinful act*.'[34] Barth has said that man as sinner is 'an inexplicable but actual absurdity'; he is, says Barth, a sinner 'on grounds or lack of grounds which are quite irrational'; we can describe a sinner but not explain his sin.[35] Emil Brunner says:

> All attempts to explain evil end in explaining it away; they end by denying the fact of evil altogether. It is of the nature of evil . . . that it should be inexplicable.[36]
> Only he who understands that sin is inexplicable knows what it is. Sin . . . is the one great negative mystery of our existence, of which we know only one thing, that we are responsible for it.[37]

Austin Farrer writes:

> Perversity is both utterly inexplicable, and perfectly simple. It is inexplicable, because it is perverse; how can you rationalize sheer unreason? It is the one irreducible surd in the arithmetic of existence. Non-rational acts, like those of blind passion, can be explained by natural causes, as can the actions of beasts. Sensible decisions are explained from the reasonable grounds which motivate them. Innocent mistakes may be explained by a mixture of the two: there are the reasonable grounds on which the mistaken man proceeds, and there is the interfering natural cause, the fatigue or the prepossession, leaving him to misinterpret them. But nothing can explain wicked perversity; nothing can explain why reason, supplied with rational grounds, should willfully falsify her own procedure in relation to them.[38]

Among philosophers, Kant said that the origin in us of moral evil is inscrutable, and that there is 'no conceivable ground from which the moral evil in us could originally have come'.[39] Berdyaev says:

> Evil being absolutely irrational, it is therefore incapable of being grasped by reason and remains inexplicable. . . . Evil represents the absolute limit of irrationality.[40]

Jankélévitch says that when one comes against moral evil,

> one cannot understand it. There is nothing there to understand. For the depths of pure wickedness are incomprehensible.[41]

Pardon, he says, personifying it,

> has not understood wicked freedom (for no one understands the incomprehensible), but it understands that there exists a wicked

freedom. . . . It understands that there exists what cannot be understood.[42]

Finally, Lonergan says:

> All that intelligence can grasp with respect to basic sin is that there is no intelligibility to be grasped. What is basic sin? It is the irrational. Why does it occur? If there were a reason, it would not be sin.[43]

This means that in the last analysis moral evil is inexcusable, as any explanation would be an excuse. Paul was not being unduly harsh when he said. 'They are without excuse' (Rom. 1.20). It is of immense importance here to note that inexcusable is not synonymous with unforgiveable – indeed, as shall be said later, what is excusable does not need to be forgiven and it is precisely the inexcusable which is the object of forgiveness.[44]

To say that moral evil is inexplicable is to use far too gentle a word. It is absurd, horrible, a violent attack on reason and goodness. It is as it were nothingness become real, the impossible become actual, darkness visible. Barth says:

> It has, therefore, no possibility – we cannot escape this difficult formula – except that of the absolutely impossible. How else can we describe that which is intrinsically absurd but by a formula which is logically absurd? Sin is that which is absurd, man's absurd choice and decision for that which is not, described in the Genesis story as his hearkening to the voice of the serpent, the beast of chaos. Sin exists only in this absurd event. . . . [If we understand sin] we lose all our desire to bring it into a final harmony with God and man. In all its forms – as enmity against God, as fratricide and as self-destruction – it is then seen as that which is out of place and will never be in place. Even the humblest being in the most obscure part of the created world fits in somewhere and has some potentiality and a God-given right of actualisation. But sin does not fit in anywhere and has no genuine potentiality and no right of actualisation.[45]

It is a force – the force of nothingness devouring being. As Hick says, when we think of Belsen and Auschwitz we are compelled to take seriously the idea of the demonic, in the sense of a force willing evil for the sake of evil, and then we have to see that in all moral evil this same force is at work.[46] T. H. Huxley, who was a rationalist, said that 'ethical nature may count upon having to reckon with a tenacious and powerful enemy as long as the world lasts'.[47]

Moreover, whereas the unorder in the universe which was considered in Chapter 3 may be lessening, this force of evil grows stronger as men develop morally and technically. Austin Farrer has said:

> It is quite unrealistic to describe the damaging part of our inheritance as the brute or the savage clinging to us, and not yet shaken off. There are vices of which the primitive, not to say the animal, is incapable. Progress in sophistication is not all progress in virtue; the corruption of the best is the worst, and the villainies of the civilized are the blackest.[48]

Evolution, then, is not only a gradual progress in perfection and order; it has brought with it also an increased power to be evil, and to destroy.

Does the force of evil ultimately emanate from some one person, the devil, with whom individual men ally themselves when they are morally evil? For centuries almost all Christians, whether Eastern or Western, Protestant or Catholic, would have answered this question affirmatively; in more recent times many have become doubtful. Whatever of that, there are deep powers of evil in man, so that Bernanos can talk of 'man's force and cruelty, the infinite resourcefulness of his guile and the ferocity of evil.'[49]

There are, it seems to me, bright mysteries and there is the dark mystery of moral evil. Bright mysteries, like the Trinity and the Incarnation, at first seem to be utterly strange, but the more we think about them the more reasonable they come to seem to us. As we study them, we feel ourselves moving into the light. Moral evil, however, seems at first to be easy to understand but the more we think about it the more incomprehensible it becomes to us until we feel almost forced to declare it to be impossible. As we study it, we feel ourselves moving into darkness, which of course is a biblical symbol for sin. Bright mysteries are in themselves perfectly intelligible, and though they surpass the grasp of our minds they are understood perfectly by God: but the dark mystery of moral evil is in itself pure unintelligibility, it does not surpass our minds but is opposed to reason as such, and God understands it even less than we do.

9

GOD AND SIN

I have distinguished between willing something directly, willing something indirectly, and not stopping something from happening; and I have said that the first two terms can be applied to spectators of actions as well as to those who perform them. The idea that God *directly* wills moral or any other evil is manifestly absurd. Also, God cannot, even as a spectator, will the occurrence of morally evil acts because of good that will come of them, any more than we, if we think that good would come of an immoral action, may wish that someone would do it. It has to be acknowledged that in the Old Testament God is sometimes said to make people commit sins: in Genesis, Joseph seems to say that God made his brothers sell him into slavery (Gen. 41.5–8) and in Exodus God is said to make Pharaoh's heart stubborn. Also, John says that the Jews could not believe because God had blinded their eyes and hardened their hearts (John 12.39–40); and II Thessalonians (which, by the way, is of doubtful authenticity) says: 'God sends upon them a strong delusion, to make them believe what is false, so that all may be condemned who did not believe the truth but had pleasure in unrighteousness' (2.11–12). Here God seems to be making people sin in order to achieve some purpose of his own, which may be to have further grounds for punishing them, which he wants to do because of their earlier sins; but the fact remains that this would be wrong and hence these texts are not to be taken entirely at face value.

God does not will moral evil *indirectly*, either, that is, in so far as it is inextricably bound up with some good that he wishes to achieve, because (unlike other kinds of unorder and unlike suffering) moral evil is not an intrinsically necessary element of the universe.

But perhaps God is responsible for sin by virtue of the fact that he created beings who are *capable* of sin? Now there is no doubt that God has caused the existence of beings who, as he presumably knew when he created them, are capable of committing morally evil acts; the question is, does this make him in any way responsible for the evil they do? First, the capacity for moral evil does not necessarily involve any moral defect such as pride or selfishness; neither does it necessarily involve any natural defect such as ignorance or slowness of mind; the only thing like this which it necessarily involves is finiteness, which is not a defect at all. Secondly, it is not wrong merely to be capable of doing wrong; evil begins with the actual morally evil decision. Therefore, if someone decides to bring into existence a being that will be capable of moral evil, there is nothing evil in the content of the decision. If there were, it would be morally evil for anyone to have a child, for every child when it grows up becomes capable of moral evil. A particular couple debating whether to have another child might say to each other: 'But it could grow up to be another Marquis de Sade or a Hitler'; they would be right, but this does not mean that it would be immoral for them to have it. Neither, then, was it immoral on God's part to create men, though we are capable of moral evil.

Suppose, however, that one asks: Is it morally right to bring into existence a being of which one knows in advance that it will actually commit grave moral evil? Suppose, for example, that the people mentioned in the preceding paragraph were to be told by a fortune-teller, 'If you have another child, he will grow up to be another Hitler', *and were to believe it*; does it not seem that it would be wrong for them to have the child? Does it not seem that if, believing what the fortune-teller had told them, they were to decide to have a child just the same, they would be assuming responsibility for dreadful evils to come? If so, then there is a difficulty in the Molinist theory, according to which God knows with absolute certainty what any possible free being would do in any situation it could possibly be in, and in the light of that knowledge decides which beings will exist and what situations they will be in. God, then, before (I am not using 'before' in a temporal sense, of course, but to denote an ante-

cedence that is purely logical[1]) creating this universe, knew that
if he created it all the moral evils that have been committed in
it would be committed. The object of his decision to bring
beings into existence, therefore, was not merely beings capable
of moral evil, but beings who definitely would exercise that
capacity and commit moral evil. It is difficult to avoid the
conclusion that if this is true, then God bears responsibility for
the morally evil acts of his creatures – a responsibility that is
increased if it is added that he could, by careful selection of free
beings and situations for them to be in, have created a universe
free of moral evil. For my part, however, I have maintained that
free decisions are intrinsically unknowable until actually made,
so that even God cannot know with certainty what a possible
free being would do in any situation.[2] According to the view put
forward in this work, then, into God's decision to create free
beings goes the knowledge that human beings are capable of sin,
and no more than that.

We come, then, to the position that God in no way positively
wills moral evil or sin, and is not at all responsible for it. He is
simply and absolutely against it, and its effects do not come
from him. When Vatican II says that man 'is engulfed by manifold ills which cannot come from his good Creator', it is evi-
dently referring primarily to the effects of sin. In scriptural
language, 'God is light and in him is no darkness' (I John 1.15);
there is no connection between God and sin.

This seems to be the clear teaching of Genesis in its account
of the sin of Adam, for according to that story God tells Adam
not to eat the fruit of the tree, then leaves him, and in God's
absence Adam sins. Adam's sin is partly explained by the fact
that Eve tempted him, her sin is likewise partly explained by the
fact that the serpent tempted her, and there the search for an
explanation stops. There is no suggestion that God was behind
the serpent, or that in any other way he had a hand in bringing
about the sin. He was against it.[3] This is also clearly the
teaching of Sirach:

> Do not say, 'The Lord was responsible for my sinning',
> For he is never the cause of what he hates.[4]

In the New Testament we have the parable of the wheat and

the darnel, where the owner of a field sows good wheat in it; when his servants later report to him that there is darnel among the wheat, he says, 'Some enemy has done this'; since the whole point of the parable would be ruined if the owner had made the enemy sow the darnel in his field, its sense is that God is not responsible for evil. But why quote such passages when from beginning to end the Bible tells of God's commandments not to sin, his warnings to men not to commit sins, his anger at them when they do, his severe judgment on sinners and the punishments he inflicts on them? This constant teaching of the Bible makes it necessary to exclude from God any will for sin or responsibility for it.

This is also the teaching of at least some of the Fathers of the church. For example, Gregory of Nyssa wrote:

> As the proper character of free-will is to choose freely the desired object, the responsibility for the ills you suffer today does not fall on God, who made us independent and free, but on your imprudence, which chose the worst instead of the best.[5]

Barth insists that God is totally opposed to sin: God, he says, says No to sin and to us when we are its representatives:

> It is a No in which there is no hidden Yes, no secret approval, no original or ultimate agreement. It is the No of the implacable wrath of God. Sin is the enemy of God, and God is the enemy of sin. Sin has no positive basis in God, no place in his being, no positive part in his life, and therefore no positive part in his will and work. It is not a creature of God. It arises only as the exponent, and in the creaturely world the most characteristic exponent, of what God has not willed and does not will and will not will, of that which absolutely is not, or is only as God does not will it, of that which lives only as that which God has rejected and condemned and excluded. When man sins, he does that which God has forbidden and does not will.[6]

Maritain, though a different kind of thinker from Barth, agrees with him about this. God, he says, causes indirectly the ills that are linked inevitably and by nature with the good things of human life, but 'as to moral evil or evil of fault, it is absolutely not willed by God or caused by him';[7] 'God is absolutely not the cause of moral evil, neither directly nor indirectly.... Every shadow of indirect causality must be excluded';[8] 'God is in no degree the inventor of the evil that the creature does, he has in no degree and in no respect the initiative of sin'.[9] 'It is man,' he says, 'who is the first cause and who has the first initiative of moral evil';[10] 'It is I who am the first cause' of evil, and 'evil as such is the only thing I am able to do without God';[11] men, he says, 'have also their share of initiative, and even their share of *first* initiative in the case where it is a question of the initiative of evil',[12] and he speaks of 'the gods from below that free agents are when they take the initiative of nothingness'.[13] Journet, who quotes Maritain's view, says that sin 'is produced by man alone, without God and against God. . . . It is man alone who takes the initiative and is the first cause of sin'.[14]

It has been said that according to this conception sin is a quasi-creation, and the term may be accepted provided that it is realized that sin is destructive and a destructive creation is a contradiction in terms. It would be better to call it an anti-creation.

God's attitude towards moral evil or sin is therefore, at most, one of not stopping it, with no element of complaisance or satisfaction. One sees it manifested, perhaps, in the account of the betrayal of Jesus by Judas. Both Luke and John say that Satan entered into Judas, and he went to the priests: whatever this means, it implies that God had no part in his action. After Judas's mind was made up, and his decision had been sealed by an arrangement with the priests, Jesus said to him: 'What you are going to do, do quickly' (John 13.27). It is as if the husband whose wife had made up her mind to leave him[15] were to say to her. 'If you are going to go, go now.' No approval whatever is implied, only a desire to be finished as soon as possible with an unpleasant business. Finally, in Acts Paul and Barnabas say that God in the past 'allowed all the nations to walk in their own ways' (14.16), and in Romans Paul says that God 'gave them up in the lusts of their hearts to impurity' (1.24). This is what I am calling 'not stopping' something.

That God does not stop sin does not, of course, mean that he is unconcerned about it. In the Bible, his reaction to it is wrath. Isaiah says that 'the name of the Lord comes from afar, burning with anger' and that the Lord will cause his majestic voice to be heard 'in furious anger' (30.27-30), and there must be a hundred passages like this in the Old Testament. In the New Testament, Jesus looks at the Pharisees in anger (e.g., Mark 3.5) and there are further references to the wrath of God in Paul and John. We, too, may react to moral evil with anger. If a person leaves his or her spouse, cruelly and without sufficient cause, to try to start life again with some younger person, the one who is left and his or her friends may feel rising within them, as they talk about what has happened, a justified anger; and when people see how the poor of the world are exploited and oppressed they may become deeply angry, as Christ became angry with the temple profiteers who were exploiting the poor. In saying this I plainly disagree with all those writers who imagine that the Christian always submits or resigns himself to evil, and cannot appreciate tragedy. 'Faith,' says Camus, 'presumes the acceptance of the mystery of evil, and resignation to injustice';[16] and David D. Raphael says that whereas tragedy 'treats evil as unalloyed evil; it regrets the waste of human worth of any kind, and does not think that innocent suffering can be justified', the religion of the Bible 'is optimistic and trusts that evil is always a necessary means to a greater good'; it 'praises submission' and 'commands resignation'.[17] Along with Rodriguez and many other Christians, they have, I believe, misunderstood Christianity.

What I have presented is a version of what is called the Free Will Defence (of God), and it excludes the idea that God can be blamed for the evil that is done in the world. It also excludes the idea that God is at work in sin itself and can be found by descending into evil.

Some authors argue as follows: a sinless universe is inherently possible; therefore if God is omnipotent he could have made a sinless universe; that is, he had a choice between sinless universes and universes with sin in them and chose to create one of the latter group; therefore those who say that God is omnipotent cannot deny that he is responsible for sin. For instance, J. L. Mackie argues against theism as follows:

> If there is no logical impossibility in a man's freely choosing the good on one, or on several, occasions, there cannot be a logical impossibility in his freely choosing the good on every occasion.

God was not, then, faced with a choice between making innocent automata and making beings who, in acting freely, would sometimes go wrong; there was open to him the obviously better possibility of making beings who would act freely but always go right.[18]

He goes on to talk of God's 'failure to avail himself of this possibility'. Those who argue in this way frequently expect theists to assert that a sinless universe is inherently impossible. Flew, for instance, says that the fundamental or key position of the Free Will Defence is 'that there is a contradiction in the suggestion that God could create a world in which men are able to do what is right or what is wrong, but in fact always choose to do what is right'.[19] That, however, is not my position. I can see no inherent impossiblity in a sinless universe, but I deny that God was (as Mackie would say) faced with a choice between creating a universe in which people sin and creating another in which they do not; I maintain that he decided to create a universe, not knowing in advance whether it was going to include sin or not.

10

THE WAGES OF SIN, AND THE
THESIS OF THIS BOOK

Sin often has some pleasant results, such as money, power, prestige or sexual pleasure, but in committing sin a man wills destruction, and destruction follows. The extent of it can be learned from life or from the Bible and great literature – including Shakespeare's tragedies, in almost all of which moral evil is the main source of the disturbed state of affairs which exists at the beginning or which comes into existence as the play proceeds, and of the suffering and deaths which occur.

First, sinners harm themselves: 'those who commit sin are the enemies of their own lives' (Tob. 12.10), and sinners 'destroy themselves by their own work of destruction'.[1] A person derives his identity from his past, his specific qualities, and his aims; if he has done evil and still wills to have done it, or if he intends to do evil, then his very identity – his 'I' or self – is evil, and he is in his own eyes unjust, cruel, vicious or bad in some other way, and therefore, repulsive and hateful. His awareness is his anguish of conscience. 'The worm of conscience still be-gnaw thy soul', is Queen Margaret's curse on Gloucester, and on the night before his death it does. He says.

> Alack! I love myself. Wherefore? for any good
> That I myself have done unto myself?
> O! no: alas! I rather hate myself
> For hateful deeds committed by myself. . . .
> My conscience hath a thousand several tongues,
> And every tongue brings in a several tale,
> And every tale condemns me for a villain. . . .

> All several sins, all us'd in each degree,
> Throng to the bar, crying all, 'Guilty! guilty'
> I shall despair.[2]

This is the voice of a totally alienated subject, at war with God, other people, society and himself as well; and by his sin he has chosen to be alienated.

It might seem that the sinner acts as a pure subject, enjoying unlimited freedom as he refuses to accept and be bound by anything, even his own nature. However, real freedom rests on an acceptance, or in Camus's words 'real freedom is an inner submission', and 'the negation of everything is in itself a form of servitude';[3] and the Bible constantly affirms that servitude is a consequence of sin – Jesus says. 'Every one who commits sin is a slave to sin' (John 8.34) and Peter says that false teachers promise freedom, 'but they themselves are slaves of corruption; for whatever overcomes a man, to that he is enslaved' (II Peter 2.19). Our ideas of salvation and redemption are based on this insight; that the sinner is not free but rather enslaved. This is shown with force in Marlowe's *Faustus*, where Faustus expects to be 'on earth as Jove is in the sky', to be 'great emp'ror of the world' and to have Mephistopheles as his slave, always obedient to his will; but once Faustus has signed his agreement with Lucifer he is refused his first request, for a wife, refused an answer to his question, 'Who made the world?', reprimanded for talking of Christ, told that if does not revolt against God Mephistopheles will in piece-meal tear his flesh, and in the end dragged screaming to hell. By committing himself to evil he hoped to obtain unlimited mastery and freedom; instead, literally, his soul was not his own and he became the slave of tyrannical evil.

Moreover, a sinner denies reason, and so destroys meaning for himself. The feeling then grows in him that

> There's nothing serious in mortality,
> All is but toys,[4]

or that everything in life is inane and meaningless. The biblical word for this is 'vanity'. The corresponding modern word is perhaps 'absurdity', and the sinner's feeling that life is absurd is powerfully expressed by Macbeth:

> Life's but a walking shadow, a poor player
> That struts and frets his hour upon the stage
> And then is heard no more. It is a tale
> Told by an idiot, full of sound and fury,
> Signifying nothing.[5]

With all this come *ennui*, *taedium vitae*, the loss of will to live, and sadness. Brunner says that 'if we had eyes to see, even in feeling we would discover the effect of sin as a fundamental joylessness, which always lies concealed under all other feelings',[6] and again I quote Macbeth. There is immense sadness in these lines:

> I have lived long enough; my way of life
> Is fallen into the sere, the yellow leaf;
> And that which should accompany old age,
> As honour, love, obedience, troops of friends,
> I must not look to have.[7]

I quote, also, from Bernanos. A character in *Joy* says:

> I too can be sad . . . with a sadness that is as cold as hell! Now that I have experienced it I shall never forget it, never! There is an intoxication in sadness, a vile intoxication! It is like foam on the lips. I have eaten of the forbidden fruit. Oh, it is horrible! . . . Sadness came into the world with Satan – that world our Saviour never prayed for, the world you say I do not know. Oh, it is not so difficult to recognize: it is the world that prefers cold to warmth! What can God find to say to those who, of their own free will, of their own weight incline towards sadness and turn instinctively towards the night?[8]

In this sadness there is trouble and fear or, to use Kierkegaard's term, there is dread. This is the opposite of the peace of Christ.

All these negative elements in the sinner's consciousness can, and frequently do, cause him to become physically sick. As Paul says, 'there will be tribulation and distress for every human being who does evil' (Rom. 2.9); or as Rahner says, sickness is an expression of sin in the sense of something which follows 'naturally' from it and at the same time is sometimes a 'sign' of sin:

> The decaying, sick body is the visible carrying out of sinful

existence. Today this is not just our theological point of view; it is increasingly also the psychological and medical point of view. Sickness is not just an accidental development; it is the connatural manifestation of the spiritual decay that is posited with sin. It is not only an external appearance, but it is also that which interiorly belongs to the situation of the sinner; it is the expression of his existential wasteland, of his exhausting falling-back-upon-himself, of his self-incarceration, of his not being able to do more, of his being delivered into the hands of strange powers, of his being banished into a suffering that can no longer be controlled by the spirit, but signifies the decaying, the recalcitrant, that which can no longer be dominated, the presence of death in us right now.[9]

I am not here maintaining that *all* sickness is a consequence of either the sick person's own sin or someone else's sin, for I have already said that, in an evolving universe, even without sin some sickness is certain to occur.[10] What I am here maintaining is that some sickness is a consequence of sin. If, to take an obvious example, a man commits a serious wrong and then, to escape his own reproaches, takes to drink or drugs and eventually becomes a sick man, his sickness is a consequence of his sin.

Death itself may come. When a person dies in old age, this is in every way natural; if he dies earlier, through nobody's fault, we regret the cutting-short of his life but know that such things happen and must be accepted as part of our lot; when, however, a person dies as a result of his own sinfulness, and when he dies in his sins, this is horrible. Of Duncan Macbeth says:

> After life's fitful fever he sleeps well,[11]

but no one says that of Macbeth himself or of Gloucester.

Let us now consider the sinner in relation to other human beings.

Friendship exists either on both sides or not at all. It therefore takes two to make a friendship, but one can break it by cancelling his commitment to love the other. If, then, two people have been friends and one seriously hurts the other, he breaks the friendship. The one who has been hurt sees this, and knows that he is no longer bound by the commitment which he had previously had. It would, by the way, be false to suppose that to obtain revenge he cancels his commitment. Revenge need not come into it. Similarly, if a husband or wife seriously hurts the other, for instance by deliberate adultery, the wronged partner regards the love-relationship as broken and hence refrains from any action that would be specifically expressive of conjugal love. In all those immoral actions, then, in which people hurt their friends or spouses, the wrongdoers cut themselves off from others.

Also, if a person does serious wrong to another person, or even to himself, he rejects the principle that respect is due to persons and hence implicitly denies respect to all human beings as persons. He has then no basis for a deep relationship with anyone, and he is alone. Camus is speaking of murder in the following passage, but it holds true of any serious wrong done to another:

> It suffices for a man to remove one single human being from the society of the living to automatically exclude himself from it. When Cain kills Abel, he flees to the desert. And if murderers are legion, then this legion lives in the desert and in that other kind of solitude called promiscuity.[12]

In sexual sins, besides the denial of respect to another person, there is often hostility towards another human being precisely as a woman or as a man, and the act expresses a rejection of woman or of man, and hence of half the human race.

Also, whereas in a moral choice a person implicitly accepts human nature, in an evil option he rejects it, declaring in effect that he does not want to be a human being. He thereby attempts to deny the given solidarity which we all have as human beings: he chooses outsiderhood.

In many sins there is, close to the surface of consciousness or even openly expressed, a rejection of such necessary institutions as the family, the law, or civil society. A criminal, for instance, lives 'outside the law' and is a foreign body within society, and in sexual sin a person rejects the family as he himself understands it. Moreover, since institutions are dead except in so far as the people who belong to them accept the human solidarity of which they are an expression, and since in any sin a person rejects human nature and this solidarity, it follows that in every sin there is, at this deeper level, a rejection of the structures that have been carefully and gradually made during many centuries, and without which civilized life could not continue.

Moreover, a person who sins sets himself against reality, and is thus estranged or alienated from being. He is also, by his own choice, alienated from God, as is vividly symbolized by Adam and Eve hiding from God in the bushes; he is estranged from the divine persons and from the community of Christians.

Besides hurting themselves, people who sin often directly hurt others: they swindle them, they cause them physical pain and even death, and they hurt them emotionally. Old Testament writers insisted that innocent people do not suffer for long, and certainly not to the ends of their lives, at the hands of the wicked; but we have all discovered, as one of Faulkner's characters did, 'that God either would not or could not – anyway, did not – save innocence just because it was innocent',[13] and the sufferings and death of the innocent Christ, which were caused by evil men, prove this beyond all doubt.

Moreover, the sins of human beings have caused our world to be corrupt or fallen. There is always a war or a threat of war somewhere, and we live with the threat of a nuclear world war hanging over us all the time. Hostility between human beings is constant, whether between people of different classes, of different races, of different religions or of different political views; and I do not mean simple opposition, but contempt and hatred stoked by repeated telling-over of atrocities. This simmers dangerously all the time, and at times breaks out in violence. Theft and dishonesty are so rife that it seems perfectly natural to us that we should lock our homes and cars if ever we leave them, and we take for granted the safeguards against fraud. Almost wherever we look a perverse eroticism, in which there is a strong element of sadism, invades our senses through our eyes and poisons our imaginations and feelings; it works against happy relationships between men and women. There is also a perverse delight in the violent destruction of human beings and things – 'violent sorrow seems a modern ecstasy'. Our world in some measure resembles Scotland under Macbeth's rule,

> where to do harm
> Is often laudable, to do good sometimes
> Accounted dangerous folly.[14]

Also, it is in some measure a world which has no morals ('right and wrong have no names'), so that in the end it is sheer power that counts. We recognize its description in Ulysses' speech in *Troilus and Cressida*, where he says that when people disregard 'degree',

> Force should be right; or rather, right and wrong –
> Between whose endless jar justice resides –
> Should lose their names, and so should justice too.
> Then every thing includes itself in power,
> Power into will, will into appetite;
> And appetite, a universal wolf,
> So doubly seconded with will and power,
> Must make perforce a universal prey,
> And last eat up himself. Great Agamemnon.
> This chaos, when degree is suffocate,
> Follows the choking.[15]

And we have all felt at some time that

> It is not we alone, it is not the house, it is not
>   the city that is defiled,
> But the world that is wholly foul;[16]

or we feel like the man who said that he was all right

> so long as I could think
> Even of my own life as an isolated ruin,
> A casual bit of waste in an orderly universe.
> But it begins to seem just part of some huge disaster,
> Some monstrous mistake and aberration
> Of all men, of the world, which I cannot put in order.[17]

Nature, too, is ruined by men's sins. In *Paradise Lost*, when Eve sinned

> Forth reaching to the fruit, she plucked, she ate!
> Earth felt the wound, and Nature from her seat,
> Sighing through all her works, gave signs of woe,
> That all was lost.[18]

and when Adam sinned

> Earth trembled in her entrails, as again
> In pangs, and Nature gave a second groan,[19]

and if some of the environmental destruction or pollution of earth, air and water is an unavoidable side-effect of industrial progress, which further developments in technology will enable us to rectify, much of it has been and is being caused by sheer greed and in full awareness of the avoidable damage that is being done. Earth had good reason to tremble when man began to sin.

Does sin hurt God? Most theologians say it does not: a sinner wants to hurt God, they say, but succeeds only in hurting himself, like someone hurling himself against a stone wall to knock it down.[20] However, if God really wants the good of human persons, and if by sin that good is prevented and, instead, positive harm is done to them, then a sinner deprives God of something he really wants and effects what God strongly does not want: he seems, then, to get at God in his will. Also, God sees his children turning against him, he sees his kingdom being prevented from coming and partly destroyed by Christ's own followers and others, and he suffers the hurt that any person experiences who offers his love, has it accepted, and is then rejected and even hated. The hurt, then, is not entirely on our side, and there is a kind of infinity in sin.

A frightful consequence of moral evil or sin is – *more* moral evil or sin.

First, it is almost a rule that a sin leads the man who commits it to commit other sins. 'The sinner,' says Ecclesiasticus, 'will heap sin upon sin' (Sir. 3.27). An affair, once started, can seem to keep going of its own accord as if it had momentum and be almost impossible to stop; and when Shakespeare's Richard III has murdered his nephews he is driven on to further crimes:

> I am in
> So far in blood, that sin will pluck on sin.[21]

Macbeth, having murdered Duncan, goes on to murder Banquo, saying:

> Things bad begun make strong themselves by ill,[22]

and later he says:

> I am in blood
> Stepped in so far, that, should I wade no more
> Returning were as tedious as go o'er.[23]

'Sin will pluck on sin': it is a law of being. Sin in a person's consciousness is like a defect in a machine, which, if it is not removed, causes undue strain to be placed on other parts of the machine so that they, too, become defective. For one thing, a decision to sin is rarely a commitment to one isolated act. More often, a series of acts is involved, and with each act a person strengthens his intention and makes himself more deeply committed to evil. Also, it often happens that by his morally evil acts a person puts himself into such a position that a tremendous effort of will would be needed for him not to go on sinning: if, for example, a man obtains a great deal of money by unjust means, and uses it to buy a beautiful house, send his children to exclusive schools and live expensively, it would almost seem to be asking too much of him to require that he impoverish himself to return the money to its rightful owners; again, if a man has a sexual liaison which he himself believes to be immoral, it may require a tremendous effort on his part to break it off; if a man is dishonest or commits adultery, he thereby commits himself to telling lies to cover what he has done, and when he tells these lies he commits himself to telling more lies later on. In such cases as these a man by sinning binds himself to sin, and almost inevitably goes from sin to sin. Again, after a man has done something which he believes to be wrong he is often strongly inclined to alleviate his sense of guilt by trying to persuade himself that what he did was not wrong after all; when he thinks he has just succeeded in doing this he will experience a strong drive to do whatever it was again, to show himself that he can do it now without compunction: and so, once more, 'sin will pluck on sin'.

Secondly, moral evil in one person leads to moral evil in others:

> The act of evil
> breeds others to follow,
> young sins in its own likeness,[24]

says Aeschylus in a trilogy in which adultery leads to war, and another adultery leads to the killing of a husband, which in turn leads to the killing of a mother by her son. Violence breeds violence; sexual vice poisons a milieu so that more sexual vice follows it; if in politics or in business people start to use 'dirty tricks', their competitors are (or claim to be) under pressure to do the same. As Bernanos says,

> every crime creates around it a sort of whirlpool which inexorably draws both the innocent and the guilty towards its vortex. It is impossible to determine in advance its strength or how long it will last. . . . An act that scarcely seems to be more important than a flick lets loose a mysterious power that rolls the criminal and the judge pell-mell in the same swirl, for as long as it has not exhausted its violence, and we do not know the laws which govern it. [25]

So strong is the pressure of sin to pluck on sin, that theologians affirm that man would necessarily sin if it were not for grace.

There exists in Christian tradition the doctrine of the Fall, and many Christians have seen in it the explanation of all the ills we experience. They have believed that the first human beings lived in paradise, enjoying a delightful harmony with God, with each other, with animals and with the rest of nature. Nothing caused them pain or anxiety, work was not a burden, childbirth caused (or would have caused) no pain, they were nude without embarrassment, they all spoke (and would have continued to speak) the same language, were never sick and they were not doomed to die. They turned against God, however, and so fell or were driven from paradise, and the reason why we find work a burden, why childbirth is painful, why we experience shame, why we speak different languages, and why we become sick and die is that these are the consequences of human wrongdoing: that is, everything that is not right with the world is an effect of sin. This idea is in the early chapters of Genesis. It is indicated in Romans, when Paul says that death came into the world and spread throughout the whole human race because of sin. Augustine explicitly extended this to *all* our ills, when he said: 'Whatever we consider to be bad is either sin or punishment for sin',[26] and this came to be taken for granted by almost all Christians. It is interesting to notice that some secular explanations of the present corrupt state of the world have a similar pattern. Rousseau, for instance, begins *Emile* with the words. 'All is well as it leaves the hands of the Author of things; everything degenerates in the hands of man'. He said that man in his primitive state, prior to the setting-up of any institutions, was perfect and happy, but that by institutions of his own invention he has become bad. He blamed the deaths caused by the Lisbon earthquake not on God or nature but on man, who had developed an unnatural civilized life which involved crowding people into great buildings so that in the earthquake many were killed. Rousseau places less emphasis on deliberate moral evil than there is in the Christian doctrine of the Fall, but the pattern of the explanation of evil is the same. One may call the Christian view the Augustinian view, after its greatest expounder.

The Teilhardian or 'Rise' theory and the Augustinian or 'Fall' theory are diametrically opposed to each other. One says that we are imperfect because we are on our rising way towards a state of perfection ahead of us in the future; the other says that our world is imperfect because it has fallen from a state of perfection that existed behind us in the past. Perhaps the Augustinian theory appeals more strongly to people with an inclination to look back, the Teilhardian one more strongly to those whose nature it is to look forward. Also, it is possible that the Augustinian view tends to have greater appeal to what I might call literary-minded theologians, since it is far more to the fore in the Bible and tradition and since it takes account, as the other does not, of moral evil. On the other hand, the Teilhardian view may appeal more strongly to scientifically-minded people, who perhaps tend to be insufficiently aware of moral evil but who are aware of the evidence upon which the theory of evolution is based and so cannot accept the Augustinian view. My contention is that, at least to a first approximation, we experience two quite different kinds of trouble, and that each of the two theories is a valid explanation of one kind but not of the other. There are such events as earthquakes, which cause tremendous damage, including the premature deaths of human beings. It seems to be perfectly natural that these should occur from time to time as the earth cools and its crust contracts, a process that has been going on since long before human beings began to exist and sin entered the world; it also seems natural that we needed time to learn how to predict earthquakes, and hence it seems natural that for a certain period of time people should have sometimes lost their lives in them. Such events and such deaths are thus neither sin nor penalty for sin. These are the shadows of my title, side-effects of light. The Augustinian theory, then, does not fit these facts. On the other hand, there is moral evil and there are its consequences: this is the dark. The Teilhardian theory, as I have said, does not account for these,[27] as of course the Augustinian theory does. It is plain, then, that instead of adopting either theory and rejecting the other we must accept both, regarding each as valid for certain phenomena only. This is the thesis of this book.

The distinction which I am making between two kinds of trouble does not exactly correspond to the distinction between physical and moral evil. and I am not maintaining that Augustine explains moral evil whereas Teilhard explains physical evil On one side of my distinction I put moral evil *and its physical consequences*; on the other side I put those troubles which occur through nobody's fault.

A particular occurrence may be both kinds of trouble at once. If, for example, a young person who has been given the best possible medical care dies of leukemia, this is in one sense nobody's fault. However, it is probable that if men had not been so sinful in the past our medical knowledge would be further advanced than it is, and that we would have discovered a cure for leukemia by now; so that to some extent the death is a consequence of sin. Fully to understand such a sad event, then, we must call on both the Teilhardian and Augustinian theories.

Of which is there more, the first kind of trouble or the second? C. S. Lewis suggested that 'human wickedness accounts for perhaps four fifths of the suffering of men';[28] if so, Augustine explains 80 per cent of our troubles and Teilhard the other 20 per cent. Most of us, I think, would say we do not have the slightest idea; but we would expect the Teilhardian proportion to be continually decreasing as evolution proceeds, and the other proportion to be continually increasing as man's power for good and evil increases.

The idea that there are two kinds of evil is not mine alone. Schleiermacher, for instance, distinguished two kinds of evil: 'the one', he said, 'is much more determined by the total forces of nature, and the other by the collective conditions of human

activity';[29] the former is independent of human action whereas
the other is due to human action.[30] This is not quite my view,
but approaching it. Barth makes a distinction between what he
calls the shadow-side (*Schattenseite*) of the universe on the one
hand and a force of annihilation (*das Nichtige*) on the other. He
speaks of 'the ills which are inseparably bound up with crea-
turely existence in virtue of the negative aspect of creation'[31] –
this is its shadow-side. But as for sin and its consequence –

> We have called sin the concrete form of nothingness [*das Nichtige*]
> because in sin it becomes man's own act, achievement and guilt.
> . . . Sin as such is not only an offence to God; it also disturbs,
> injures and destroys the creature and its nature. . . . [It is fol-
> lowed by] the suffering of evil as something wholly anomalous
> which threatens and imperils this existence and is no less incon-
> sistent with it than sin itself. . . . Nor is it a mere matter of dying as
> the natural termination of life, but of death itself as the life-des-
> troying thing to which all suffering hastens as its goal, as the
> ultimate irruption and triumph of that alien power which
> annihilates creaturely existence and thus discredits and disclaims
> the Creator. There is real evil and real death as well as real sin.
> . . . That nothingness [*das Nichtige*] has the form of evil and death
> as well as sin shows us that it is what it is not only morally but
> physically and totally. It is the comprehensive negation of the
> creature and its nature.[32]

PART FOUR

THE REMEDY FOR MORAL EVIL

REPENTANCE

It might seem to be impossible to remedy moral evil, for once a person has done wrong the fact remains for ever that he has done it. As Lady Macbeth says, 'What's done is done' and 'What's done cannot be undone'. Moreover, all that a man has done makes up *his* past, which sticks to him always, so that as Faulkner says 'The past is never dead. It's not even past,'[1] and if there are evil deeds in that past they remain on, poisoning the present and waiting to poison the future as soon as it arrives, so that it seems as if once a man has done wrong he will never again be innocent and clean, or enjoy a good conscience. He will always have to say, like Harry in *The Family Reunion*,

> I am the old house
> With the noxious smell and the sorrow before morning,
> In which all past is present, all degradation
> Is unredeemable.[2]

What should a person do, then, if he has committed an evil act? Stand by it proudly, says Sade. 'Let's not cry over spilt milk; remorse is inefficacious, since it does not stay us from crime, futile since it does not repair it, therefore it is absurd to beat one's breast',[3] and remorse 'merely denotes an easily subjugated spirit'.[4] Despair, say others; and many people do feel they will never be free of the burden that presses on them because of some wrong they have done.

To say, however, that because the past deed cannot be undone, therefore the moral guilt remains forever, is to confuse the objective and subjective orders. It is true that the actual act of choice and any deeds in which it was realized are past and as such unchangeable; but it is also true that in so far as they are past they no longer exist. However, when a person makes any choice he normally wills afterwards to have made it[5] and when a person makes an evil decision he 'normally' continues for the rest of his life to will to have made it, so that at any moment of his later life there is an immoral volition existing in the present: it is this, a moral evil poisoning a person's heart in the present and threatening to go on poisoning it in the future, which causes us to say that evil deeds live on or that when someone has done evil he goes on for ever being evil – this abiding will-to-have-done-what-he-did is what constitutes the part of the problem of evil we are considering at the moment. Now because the object of this volition (the past deed) considered in itself cannot be changed, it does not follow that nothing can be done about the volition, a subjective reality existing now.

One might think that a resolution not to commit moral evil in future would suffice to cleanse a person of guilt, but a person could very well say, 'I am glad I did what I did and I shall always remember it with great satisfaction, though I know it was wrong; however, once was enough and I shall not do it again.' There is no inconsistency in that, and since this person is clearly here and now morally evil because of his present attitude towards his own past deed, we must conclude that a resolution concerning the future does not of itself remove existing moral evil.

People sometimes try to free themselves from guilt by telling themselves – or listening to someone else telling them – that it is useless to worry about the past, and that they must forget it and think only of the present and future. However, it is simply not in our power to erase our memories as we can erase the memories of computers; we can never forget important events in our lives, however hard we try.

If in principle the will to have done evil remains in a person's heart unless something is done about it, a condition for achieving freedom from moral evil must be the intellectual act of admission of guilt: a person who has sinned must say. 'I ruined such and such a person's reputation (or whatever the wrong action was). I knew at the time it was wrong, but I freely chose to do it. In so doing I broke away from God. I, who am speaking now, did an evil thing, and I am responsible for its evil consequences. I am guilty.' He must not act like the adulteress:

> This is the way of an adulteress:
> she eats, and wipes her mouth,
> and says, 'I have done no wrong' (Prov. 30.20),

but like David, who said:

> I acknowledged my sin to thee,
> and I did not hide my iniquity;
> I said, 'I will confess my
> transgressions to the Lord' (Ps. 32.5).

The admission of guilt will not alone suffice to remedy moral evil, for a person could choose to stand by his deed, saying: 'I know it was wrong, but I am glad I did it and would do it again', in which case the admission of guilt would lead only to an intensification of the will to be evil and an increase of guilt. There must come, after the admission of guilt, an act of the will which is exactly opposed to the volition to have done something which one did in the past. The person must say. 'I wish I had not done what I did.' However, just as it is immoral to decide that one definitely would do something wrong if it were not for purely practical difficulties,[6] so also one continues to be immoral if one looks back on an immoral action and decides that, because of practical disadvantages it turned out to have and only because of them, one wishes one had not done it. (A married man who decides that he definitely would take another woman to a hotel for a night if it would not cost so much money, is unfaithful at heart; and so is a man who did that and now wishes he had not done so, because of how much money it cost him.) Consequently, to cancel a morally bad abiding intention a person who has done wrong must say. 'I wish I had not done what I did, because it was wrong', or 'because it hurt other persons', or 'because it offended God'. With this volition, guilt is removed, moral evil ceases to exist, and a bad person becomes a good one.[7] It is called repentance, or sorrow for sin.

It is clear that repentance has the form of a wish, that this wish cannot possibly be fulfilled, and that the person who makes it knows when he makes it that it cannot come true. It might seem, then, to be a completely futile act, such as no one could possibly make with full seriousness. However, if one thinks of a man wishing that the woman he loved had not died, or that she had not married someone else, one realizes that a person can make a wish with the utmost seriousness, and can put into it the full force of his will, even though he knows that it cannot come true. Again, if one thinks of a person who deeply hates another, who sees that that other person has achieved some success, and who with a burning intensity of will-power wishes that that success had been denied, one sees once more that an unrealizable wish can totally engage a person. It does not at all follow, therefore, that because what is done cannot be undone, therefore the wish not to have done something cannot be strong. As for the wish being futile, the usefulness of a volition is not to be measured only by the changes it effects in the objective order, for some very important volitions are concerned not with producing, changing or removing some objective reality but with fixing the subject's attitude towards some reality which in itself is unaffected by the volition: for instance, a man who has been born with a deformity can maintain an attitude of acceptance towards it, or alternatively he can put his strength of will into maintaining an attitude of bitter resentment of it, and – far from being futile – the volition he chooses to make will determine whether he is a contented or miserable man.

Repentance is not synonymous with regret. After all, one can regret the fact that it rained, or that one was not born in the eighteenth century, but one cannot repent of these facts. Furthermore, one can regret a past action of one's own without repenting of it. It is not synonymous with shame, either, for a man can be ashamed of the poverty of his parents, of his own poverty, or for that matter of being rich, without seeing any moral fault in what he is ashamed of. It has been suggested that repentance is a form of fear – that as children we were punished when we did wrong, and so were conditioned to experience fear after doing wrong, and this fear is repentance or the motive for it. However, as Scheler says, a person actually needs to be relatively free of fear in order to be alone with himself and his deed, reflect on it and wish not to have done it because it was wrong; moreover, fear makes a person look forward, whereas in repentance one looks back; finally, a person repents from the centre of his being, but fear comes over him from without.[8] According to Scheler, Adam Smith suggested that repentance is the sinner's sympathy with the desire of others to take revenge on him. This would make the desire to take revenge on another when he does evil the primary fact, and a sinner's own repentance a derived phenomenon. But, says Scheler, reflection on experience shows that the latter is at least as primary as the former.[9] Repentance is not a kind of spiritual hang-over, or state of depression caused by the unpleasant after-effects of an evil deed, since in despair this exists without repentance. Finally, repentance is not a form of masochistic self-torture, for it produces beneficial results.

At times repentance is easy, as when a person, in a moment of weakness – but still in the possession of his faculties and responsible for his actions – does something that is mean or spiteful, or out of cowardice betrays his own principles, then within a short time and quite spontaneously acknowledges his fault and repents of what he has done. At other times, however, repentance is very difficult. Suppose, for instance, that a woman falls deeply in love with a married man, becomes his devoted mistress and for years lives only for him, though believing all the time that what she is doing is wrong. Suppose, then, that eventually the man dies. One might think that the way is now open to her to free herself from guilt by repentance, but it may be no easier to say, 'I wish I never made love with him' after his death than it would have been to break off the relationship with him before it. Told to repent of what she has done, the woman may reply. 'But he was my life. For me to say, "I wish I had not become his mistress" would be like destroying my life. I feel as though you are asking me to kill myself.' Well, this is surely what 'dying to one's old self' or 'dying to sin' means: by repentance one disconnects oneself personally from a part of one's past life, or ends a life one has been living with commitment; and if the wrong-doing has been a large part of one's life for a long time and if one was deeply committed to it, then this is not at all easy. Often, indeed, a person may have to think about what he has done and face the evil of it for a long time before he can finally repent of it.

When repentance clears away present evil, we are immediately free to go forward with energy and hope. As Scheler says, repentance has, 'together with, and even in consequence of, its negative, demolishing function, another which is positive, liberating and constructive';[10] repentance, he says, drives the deed with its root out of the living centre of the self, 'and thereby enables life to begin . . . a new course springing forth from the centre of the personality which, by virtue of the act of repentance, is° no longer in bonds'.[11]

Well may the plain man say, 'No regrets! – just resolve to do better in future'. But what the plain man fails to tell us is where we may find strength to make these resolutions, still less the strength to carry them out, if Repentance has not first liberated the personal Self and empowered it to combat the determining force of the past.[12]

Repentance, at least in its perfect form, genuinely annihilates the psychic quality called 'guilt'. And so it bursts the chain of evil's reproductive power which is transmitted through the growth in evil of men and times. This then is the way in which it enables men to embark on new and guiltless courses.

Repentance is the mighty power of self-regeneration of the moral world, whose decay it is constantly working to avert. There lies the great paradox of Repentance, that it sorrowfully *looks* back to the past while *working* mightily and joyfully for the future, for renewal, for release from moral death.[13]

And so Ezekiel says. 'If a wicked man turns away from all his sins which he has committed and keeps all my statutes and does what is lawful and right, he shall surely live; he shall not die' (Ezek. 18.21).

Therefore, even though Lady Macbeth is right when she says, 'What's done cannot be undone'; even though we cannot relive any part of our past lives and get it right the second time; even though the cherubs with the flaming swords prevent us from going *back* to the garden of Eden; nevertheless an evil deed committed in the past is not irreparable. Repentance causes it to cease fouling the present, prevents it from spoiling the future, and frees us to go *forward* to paradise.

12

FORGIVENESS[1]

By committing sin a person not only puts evil in his own heart but also alienates himself from other persons, and we must now examine what needs to be done for his relationships with them to be restored. The relationships which I shall have primarily in mind are those of deep married love and close friendship, but what is said of these will hold for friendships that are not very close, for what might be called good acquaintanceships and for relationships between individual wrong-doers and communities to which they have belonged. I shall also be considering the restoring of the relationships between a sinner and the divine persons. The problem we face now is this: if two people have loved each other and knowingly and deliberately one of them has grievously wronged and hurt the other, thus breaking off their love-relationship, what is needed for them to love one another again?

Should the person who has been hurt put his mind to *understanding* the offence committed against him, since if he understands it he will excuse it?

It does sometimes happen that one person appears to harm another either in his own person or in his interests, the second person concludes that the first one has deliberately turned against him, and he ceases to regard him as a friend; then he realizes that the first person never intended to hurt him, and at once regards the friendship not as restored but as never having been broken: here understanding has removed the estrangement. Or something like this happens: while a man is far away from his home on business, his eighteen-year-old son is given an opportunity to go mountain-climbing and a decision must be made at once; the mother, fearful of the risks involved but saying to herself that it would be unfair to say no to the boy because of her own womanly fears, reluctantly allows him to go, and he is killed. If now the father on his return blames the mother because she let the boy attempt a mountain which (as he, the father, would have known) was beyond his powers; if he holds her responsible for the boy's death and acts almost as if she were guilty of murdering the boy whom he calls 'my' son; and if he tells her he will never forgive her: then he seriously wrongs his wife. In such a situation, forgiveness simply is not called for. What he clearly ought to do is let her explain how she came to give the permission, understand and accept the explanation, assure the poor woman that he does not reproach her and that she must not reproach herself, and do all he can to help her sustain the loss they have both suffered.

In this example there was no fault at all in the original action, and once this is understood there is no problem. There are many other cases in which there is fault, but not as much as at first appears; in these cases understanding has the effect of showing not that no problem exists but that it is smaller than had been at first supposed.

But where there *is* moral fault, what then? 'Tout comprendre, c'est tout pardonner' has become a sort of proverb, but the trouble with moral evil is that it cannot be understood.[2] Indeed, the more one studies it, the more unintelligible it seems until one is almost ready to declare that it cannot possibly exist. It is therefore inexcusable,[3] and if one person has been evilly hurt by another there is no hope that by *understanding* what has been done to him he will be able to excuse it and so be free of his sense of hurt and open to reunion with the other.

If an offended person cannot excuse an act perhaps he can make up his mind never to mention it, to try not to think about it again, and, in a word, to let bygones be bygones; and perhaps if he does this he can be reconciled with the person who wronged him? Well, as Jankélévitch says, an extremely superficial person, for whom only the recent past, the present and the near future are real, may be able to go through life continually putting hurts and grievances aside, dismissing any thought of injuries that were done to him in the past simply on the ground that it was in the past that they were done, and being willing to associate with people who have injured him provided it was not within the previous few days: such a person may be able to say he will let bygones be bygones and mean that what happened in the past has no significance for him in the present. However, a deeper person does not let his life flow by him into nothingness, but keeps his past; for such a person 'the past is never dead – it's not even past', and to deny the present relevance of past deeds merely on the ground that they were performed in the past would be here and now to betray the values affirmed or denied in those deeds. For instance, if a woman were to say: 'My husband was unfaithful, but because it happened last week' – or last month or last year – 'it does not matter to me now', she would be untrue to her own ideal of marriage. Also, one must agree that they are in the right, those Jewish people for whom the fact that it all happened in the past is not a valid reason for dismissing from their minds all that was done to Jews in Nazi Germany; they believe, and are right in believing, that to let bygones be bygones and accept the German people indiscriminately *simply on the ground that it is all now behind us in time* would be wrong. The reason for the refusal to let bygones be bygones is that, when a man does something, he afterwards (unless he repents) goes on willing to have done it;[4] hence, though a deed itself may recede into the past, the intention of which it is the object continues to exist in the will of the agent and makes it impossible to accept him now simply on the grounds that it happened in the past. 'Let bygones be bygones' is easy to say, but the trouble is that (unless the agent repents) the intention involved in the deed is *not* bygone, and it is precisely this that is the obstacle to reunion.

But possibly time, which wears down even mountains and is said to heal all wounds, will eventually heal the offended person's sense of hurt and grievance and make a reunion possible? Well, time does have an effect. Anger subsides, for few can maintain a high pitch of anger for years. The shock one received when the offence was committed, or when one first heard of it, does not last, for one becomes accustomed to knowing what happened. What at first drove all other thoughts out of one's mind becomes gradually something that one calls to mind only now and then, and whereas for some time nothing could give one any pleasure, eventually one began to enjoy life again.

However, for a deep person nothing is changed substantially by mere time. The state, it is true, separates a criminal from society for a certain period of time and then accepts him back when he has 'done his time'; but if one hurts another person one cannot return after so many days or years, claim to have 'done one's time' and demand that the old relationship be resumed. Different principles apply.

Finally, though Vatican II said that Moslems and Christians should 'forget the past'[5] and be friends, forgetfulness cannot be the way to mend broken relationships, for people simply cannot forget serious events in their lives. As I said earlier, Jankélévitch remarks that superficial people may cease to care about what has happened to them once it has receded a little way into the past; he adds. 'Those who preach forgetfulness are only seeking to exploit people's frivolousness, laziness and superficiality.'[6]

But let us now see how a broken relationship *can* be mended. One thing that is clear from what I have been saying is that as a general rule the offence that did the damage must not simply be ignored: it must be faced squarely. This usually means that it must be talked about, however painful it may be for both parties even to mention it. To test this statement let us imagine a drama as follows.

A man who had been living in Melbourne with a very good wife and children one day left them and went with another woman to live in Sydney. After some years she left him, and he then lived by himself in Sydney. One day he met a man whom he had known in Melbourne, and who still knew his wife, and he told this man he would like to return to her – 'But,' he asked, 'would she take me back?' The friend put this question to the wife and she said yes, she would. The friend passed this information on to the man in Sydney, who sent a telegram to tell his wife he was coming and that evening flew down to Melbourne and went out to what had been their home. Much to his surprise she met him at the door as if he had never been away but was returning home from work, and as she had always done in the past proceeded to tell him the most recent news about their friends and about what she had been doing during the day. After some time of this he tried to bring up the painful subject of his desertion and adultery, but she took no notice and went on talking of other things. Eventually he understood that he could stay, but what he had done was not to be talked about or even obliquely referred to.

It seems to me that if one imagines first that one is the husband and then that one is the wife in this story, one senses that they are not going to achieve a genuine reconciliation. The past cannot be ignored like that, and it is now the wife who, by refusing to talk about it, is preventing a genuine reunion from taking place.

However, merely talking about the past obviously will not reunite people, and so we come to the next step: the wrongdoer must admit his guilt, repent of what he did and express this to the one whom he has offended. In Jeremiah we read: 'Each man will turn from his evil way, and *then I can* forgive them their misdeeds and their sin';[7] and in Luke: 'If your brother sins, rebuke him, and *if he repents*, forgive him; and if he sins against you seven times in the day, and *turns to you seven times, and says,* "*I repent*", you must forgive him' (Luke 17.3–4). Scheler, then, is quite biblical when he says that the act of repentance is required for the victim, after receiving compensation, to forgive;[8] so is Journet when he says, 'Sin without repentance *cannot* be pardoned, any more than God can annihilate himself';[9] so, finally, is John G. McKenzie when he says. 'Repentance is the condition of forgiveness'.[10] The offended person must require repentance of the other not in order to get revenge by making him undergo a painful humiliation, but because unless he repents of what he did he is still willing the hurt he caused, and such a will makes a true reunion impossible. If a man who was once my friend deliberately circulated calumnies about me in order to prevent my obtaining a position that he wanted for himself; and if later his attitude is that he is basically glad he did that and would do it again if he were able to live that part of his life over again; then I simply cannot say to him, 'I'll be your friend again' – because of an obstacle which is in his heart, not in mine. A woman whose husband has a mistress cannot accept the situation and act as if she is happily married to a man who loves her as a husband should: neither can a woman do that if her husband intends to make a certain woman his mistress at some time in the future; and, finally, a woman cannot do it if her husband had a mistress at some time in the past and is glad he did. All of which means that in saying that an offended person must require repentance of the other before reuniting with him, I am not recommending an attitude of self-righteousness, vengefulness or bitterness: I am only pointing out that repentance is necessary for a reunion and the offended person must recognize this fact.

Possibly – I am not so certain about this – for the relationship to be restored the wrongdoer must do more than express repentance: perhaps he must also ask for forgiveness. Certainly, because the person who was wronged ceased at that time to belong to or be committed to his former friend, a change in the latter's attitude does not suffice to restore the relationship. If it is to come into being again, the person who has been hurt must accept the other again, recommit himself to the relationship or give himself once more to the other. This act is forgiveness, and its characteristics correspond closely to those of love.

To love another person is to consent to him for his sake, and not – for example – in order to be a loving person; and to forgive someone is to accept him back for his sake, and not in order to be a forgiving person or for any other motive that has direct reference to oneself. Also, in love one attends to another person as a subject: it is not precisely his qualities that one is concerned with, but his thoughts and even more his intentions; and in forgiveness one is attentive to the other person's intentions – his repentance, and his will to commit himself anew to oneself.

In love one is concerned with another person as here and now present. In exercising forgiveness, too, one is concerned directly with another person as he is now: one requires of him that he be not now willing to have done what he did but that on the contrary he wish not to have done it, one sees that here and now he wants to be one's friend again, and one agrees to re-establish the relationship. That is, one's whole attention is fixed on the present state of the other's will. In this as in other ways forgiving differs from excusing, for if someone wants me to excuse some past action of his which caused me harm, I listen while he tells me what he did not know at the time or what pressures were acting on him then; if, however, someone wants me to forgive him some past action, I listen while he tells of his present repentance:

that is, to excuse a man I must make a judgment on his state of mind at some time in the past, whereas to forgive someone I must believe what he tells me about his present intentions. Also, the fact that in exercising forgiveness I am concerned with another person's present intentions means that while I must believe that here and now he intends never to hurt me again, I do not have to be sure that he will at no future time change his mind and hurt me again: a judgment about present intentions, not about future facts, is what I must make in order to be able to forgive.

Love cannot have as its motive a desire to improve the person who is loved, though an intention to help another person improve himself may sometimes exist in consciousness along with love. Similarly, it would not be forgiveness if one 'forgave' another person only in order to cause him to repent of what he had done or to reform his behaviour – anyone who says, 'If we let him off this time I'm sure he won't do it again, so let's do that' is not proposing forgiveness properly so called, firstly because forgiveness is not the same thing as 'letting off' from punishment, and secondly because of the motive proposed.[11]

There is, of course, an important difference between love and forgiveness, besides the fact that love is the making or maintaining and forgiveness is the restoring of a relationship; it consists in this, that forgiveness has what might be called an indirect object – one forgives someone *something*. The specific indirect object of forgiveness is an inexplicable, inexcusable morally evil deed. It is true that in Luke's gospel Jesus says of the soldiers who crucify him: 'Father, forgive them; for they know not what they do.' Dare one say that this is imprecise, and that a more exactly-worded prayer would have been: 'Father, excuse them'? Perhaps a better idea of forgiveness emerges from the parable of the prodigal son, where the father does not say: 'After all, it is not easy to be a younger son. Naturally enough, resentment at being in the second place built up in him until he needed to leave home to be free of the tension. I suppose also that hearing himself always referred to as my younger son made it hard for him to feel he was growing up and he felt that in order to find himself as a person in his own right he had to go far away from his brother and me. I should have seen his problem and paid more attention to him: it is all very under-

standable when I look back on it.' No, the father does not seek
to explain and excuse his son's action; but he forgives him for it.
The fact is that where a valid excuse exists for some action it
does not need to be forgiven, and it is where excusing stops that
forgiveness begins. This has been put forcibly by Jankélévitch,
who says:

> A forgiver does not require of a fault that it be attenuated by
> circumstances. This, of course, is not to say that he looks for
> aggravating circumstances; but he is not deterred by aggravation
> of the fault. To have condemned a fault in no way prevents him
> from forgiving it – on the contrary. A forgiver is not 'indulgent'.
> Rather, he is, or at any rate has been, severe.[12]

When the excuser, he says, reaches the inexcusable, he can do
nothing with it, but 'the inexcusable is what forgiveness is
concerned with, for the inexcusable is forgivable'.[13] By 'the
inexcusable', he says, we do not mean that for which we can at
the moment see no excuse, but for which we think an excuse
might eventually come to light: that is, forgiveness does not
mean giving someone the benefit of the doubt about his guilt.
'The inexcusable' which is the indirect object of forgiveness is
that for which we believe no excuse is possible.[14] He says:

> When a crime can be neither justified nor explained nor under-
> stood; when, after all that is understandable in it has been
> understood, its atrociousness and the overwhelming evidence of
> responsibility are plain for all to see; when there are no attenuating
> circumstances nor excuses of any kind. . . . then there is nothing
> to do but forgive.[15]

Love is a gift of oneself to another, and one of the characteristics of a gift is that it is something to which the recipient
does not have a strict right in justice – it would, for instance, be
wrong and indeed offensive for an employer to pretend, as he
paid his employees their wages, that they were receiving gifts
from him. Now when a person has a complete excuse for something he has done, he clearly has a right to have his excuse
considered dispassionately, judged valid and accepted: in
accepting the excuse 'one does not', says Jankélévitch, 'give him
a present or still less an alms', 'one bestows no favour on him
for he has no need of favour or charity; one simply grants him

what in justice is due to him'.[16] Excusing, then, is not a form of giving. When, however, a person has no excuse for what he has done, then even after he has repented he has no strict right to a resumption of the relationship which he broke off – for example, after men have sinned, if they later repent this does not give them a strict right to God's forgiveness – so that forgiveness is a gift in the full sense of the word and God's forgiveness is a new gift over and above the original gift of grace.

Another characteristic of a gift is that it is disinterested, and forgiveness, like love, is disinterested. If, therefore, a woman were to be abandoned by her husband, if he were later to return to her repentant and ask her forgiveness, and if she were to 'forgive' him because she needed his help with the children or because she would be better off financially, this would not be forgiveness. Also, if she were to say to herself, 'Who knows? One day I may do the same to him as he did to me, and later find myself asking for forgiveness as he is now asking me for it; so to make sure of getting it when it is my turn I will grant it to him now', this would not be genuine forgiveness because it would not be a gift but the first half of a fair exchange regulated by considerations of justice. One forgives another, then, not for any advantage to oneself but out of sheer goodwill towards the other person.

Any gift requires generosity, but forgiveness needs it even more than love does in ordinary circumstances, for like repentance it can be extremely difficult. Once bitten, twice shy. It is one thing to entrust oneself to someone who has shown one nothing but understanding and sympathy, and of whose present sincerity and future fidelity one has no reason to be suspicious; it is another thing to entrust oneself again to someone by whom, after one had given oneself the first time, one's trust had been betrayed and by whom one's happiness had been destroyed. Also, a person who has been hurt may have come almost to cherish his grievance and pain; having found himself cast in the role of sufferer, he may have lived the part so intensely that he can hardly imagine himself in any other, and hence be unwilling to relinquish it; moreover, he may hear himself saying, 'Now I can take my revenge by saying no'. Forgiveness, then, always demands generosity and it may call into being a greatness of heart that is magnificent.

It is not of the essence of giving that it involves loss for the giver; for example, one can give information – and this can be a very real form of gift – without losing it, and one gives attention, sympathy, advice and many other things without suffering loss. The gift of oneself which one makes in love is one that in principle involves no loss for the giver, and the same is true of the gift of forgiveness. In this respect forgiveness is very different from condoning, which involves a loss of integrity. As Jankélévitch says, 'forgiveness does not require of us the sacrifice of our selfhood'.[17]

Love is sometimes said to be quite inexplicable.[18] Jaspers, for instance, says that it is incomprehensible and groundless. 'I do not know objectively what I love and why';[19] and Jankélévitch, after saying that a person is loved 'because he is who he is', goes on: 'What kind of a reason is that? Well, it is just the absence of a reason which is the reason.'[20] However, since every person has value in himself, every person is himself the adequate reason for any love he receives: it is not quite true, then, that love has no explanation; what is true is that it has no reason other than the person loved. The same is true of forgiveness: one forgives another person for his sake. Again we find a difference between excusing and forgiving, for whereas excusing is essentially an intellectual judgment based on a study of facts, forgiving is a volitional act motivated by the inherent value of a person.

Since excusing is an intellectual judgment based on a study of facts, it is not in principle free. That is, if someone committed no fault when he did something that appeared to be an offence against me, when he makes his explanation and I see that it is valid I have no choice but to accept it. If, however, someone has deliberately hurt me, after I have seen that he is sincerely repentant I have a choice to make: I can forgive him or not. Whereas it would be irrational to say, 'Your excuse is valid but I will not accept it', since this would be like saying, 'I know that today is Tuesday but I refuse to believe it', it would be not irrational or unjust to say: 'Your repentance is sincere, but I will not forgive you'. Forgiveness, then, is a free act, like love.

Of its nature, forgiveness is forever; one cannot say, 'I will forgive you for a month', any more than one can say to someone, 'I will be your friend for a month'. Also, it is total. Where a person has committed a number of what seem to be offences, and offers excuses for them, one can at times quite reasonably accept some of the excuses and not others; but forgiveness, like love, is directed towards the person in his indivisible selfhood, so that one cannot forgive him for some offences while refusing to forgive him for others – one either forgives him for everything (assuming that he is sorry for everything) or one does not forgive him at all.

Does forgiveness bring with it the forgetting of the offence? There exists the phrase, 'forgive and forget', which seems to imply that if one forgives one also forgets, and in Isaiah we read:

> I am He who blots out your transgressions . . .
> I will not remember your sins. (Isa. 3.25).

However, I submit that if a person has been badly hurt by someone he loved he simply cannot forget what has happened; I submit also that God cannot forget anything, and that he has certainly not forgotten the crucifixion of his son. It seems to me, indeed, that the idea that if one forgives one also forgets has caused much needless anxiety, for it causes people to say: 'I thought I had forgiven but I find I have not forgotten, so apparently I have not forgiven after all.' Forgiveness, I suggest, is an abiding intention by virtue of which the memory of the evil deed is not obliterated but does not disturb the renewed relationship. As Temple Drake says in Faulkner's *Requiem for a Nun*.

> Love, but more than love too: . . . tragedy, suffering, having suffered and caused grief; having something to have to live with even then, because you knew both of you could never forget it. And then I began to believe . . . that there was something even better, stronger, than tragedy to hold two people together: forgiveness.[21]

In love, two persons meet on a footing of equality and mutually give themselves to each other and accept each other. In forgiveness, however, two persons seem not to meet as equals, for one is in the right and the other in the wrong; and the act is not mutual, for only one of them forgives. However, there is a certain mutuality in the two acts of repentance and forgiveness,

and they put the offender back in the right and raise him again
to a level of equality with the person he offended. A person who
forgives another does not thereby lord it over him or savour a
delicious sense of moral superiority: on the contrary, he removes
the inequality that has existed and greets the other as once more
his equal. There is therefore no humiliation in accepting
forgiveness – on the contrary, one's dignity is restored.

By forgiveness a relationship of love comes to exist between
two people which is not an entirely new relationship, for all that
they knew of each other before their separation, all they said
and did together and all that they used to mean to each other is
brought to life again in their minds and hearts and affects the
way they regard each other now. If people were old friends
before they broke apart, they become old friends when the
breach is healed. On the other hand, a relationship is made by
its history and a serious breach followed by reconciliation
cannot leave it qualitatively unchanged. What exists after the
reconciliation, then, is neither a brand-new relationship nor the
old one exactly as it used to be, but the old one qualitatively
changed.

It sometimes happens that after an entire experience of
offence, break-up, repentance, forgiveness and reunion, a
relationship is better than it was before. The partner who
did wrong may have been self-righteous before his fall and
he may now be cured of this fault with the result that the
relationship is better; or the innocent partner may have
been naive to a fault and may now be wiser, more mature
and more interesting. However, we have no right to generalize
on the basis of such cases as these. It is true that to have a deep
relationship people need both to enjoy themselves and to suffer
together; they need both to work and to play, to laugh and to
weep, together; they need perhaps sometimes to find themselves
surprisingly at one in their judgments and wishes, as if they were
thinking and deciding as one person, but also at other times to
encounter disagreements, differences in temperament, misunderstandings and clashes of mood. I cannot believe, however,
that it can be true in general that it helps if one of them mali-
ciously hurts the other, even if he later repents and is forgiven.
It also seems to me that even if in a particular case someone
could see that by deliberately hurting someone who loved him,

causing a break in the relationship, then later repenting and obtaining forgiveness, he could bring about a deepening of the relationship, it would not be right for him to do this. The end does not justify the means, and moral evil is not something that can be taken as if it were medicine: it is *evil*, and moreover it is incalculable. Only someone with an incredibly superficial sense of sin could possibly think of trying to use it to achieve some good purpose. I do not even think that it is right after the event, if a relationship has been deepened by an experience of sin and reconciliation, to be glad that the sin was committed, for this is retrospectively to will evil for the good that came of it, thus willing evil as a means to good.[22]

I have already said that forgiveness is a free act, in the sense that if someone refuses to forgive a person who has offended him and is now repentant he neither acts irrationally nor refuses to give the other what is his just due. However, if God forgives the repentant sinner and loves him, we cannot both love God and refuse to forgive the person whom he has forgiven: that is, not reason and not a right vested in the person who has offended us but our love of God obliges us to forgive whoever has offended us if he repents and asks forgiveness. Our forgiveness, then, is a free gift, and nevertheless we recognize the obligation of which Christ spoke when he told us to forgive up to 'seventy times seven times' – that is, *ad infinitum* – and which he implied when he told us to say that we forgive all those who trespass against us.

CONCLUSION

If, then, there are two radically different kinds of trouble, each has its own explanation or its own way of being inexplicable, each calls for a different emotional response, and to each there corresponds a different remedy – work and, when all else fails, dignified acceptance in the one case, repentance and forgiveness in the other. If some pages of this book have seemed depressing, and if I have seemed to demolish hopes grounded in divine omnipotence and providence as these are often understood, I hope that the final result of reading it will be peace and confidence.

NOTES

Throughout the notes a reference in brackets immediately following the title of a work [*The Symbolism of Evil* (1.26)] refers back to the original mention of that work.

Part One: Extreme Optimism and Pessimism

Chapter 1: Optimism

1. P. Geach, *Providence and Evil*, Cambridge University Press 1977, p. 58.

2. From a Christmas sermon, quoted in A. Lovejoy, 'Milton and the Paradox of the Fortunate Fall' in Lovejoy, *Essays in the History of Ideas*, Baltimore: Johns Hopkins Press 1948, p. 291.

3. 'Treatise on Conformity to the Will of God', ch. 22.

4. Soames Jenyns, *A Free Inquiry into the Nature and Origin of Evil*, London: Dodsley 1758, p: 86.

5. *Samson Agonistes*, last speech of Chorus.

6. *An Essay on Man*, I, lines 51–52, 289–294.

7. A.-D. Sertillanges, *Le problème du mal*, Paris 1948, II, 50.

8. K. Jaspers, *Tragedy Is Not Enough*, London: Gollancz 1953, p. 38.

9. U. Ellis-Fermor, *Frontiers of Drama*, London: Methuen 1964, p. 17.

10. J. Hick, *Evil and the God of Love*, London: Macmillan 1966, p. 280.

11. Quoted in Lovejoy, 'Milton and the Paradox of the Fortunate Fall', p. 292. The idea that the Fall was fortunate was expressed in the fourth century by Ambrose, who said that God 'knew that Adam would fall, in order that he might be redeemed by Christ. Fortunate disaster (*felix ruina*), which when remedied leads to something better. (*In Ps 39*, § 20: *PL*, 14, 1065.) Gregory the Great said that without Adam's sin there would have been no Incarnation, and 'who of the

elect would not willingly endure still worse evils, rather than not have so great a Redeemer?' (*In Primum Regum Expositiones*, 4, 7: *PL*, 7,222). But probably the most influential source of the idea has been the *Exultet*, a poetic and musical highlight of the old Latin liturgy, which said that the sin of Adam was 'certainly necessary' and put the phrase *felix culpa* into circulation.

12. Augustine, *Encheiridion*, ch. 26, § 100.

13. C. Journet, *The Meaning of Evil*, London: Geoffrey Chapman 1963, pp. 103–104.

14. Geach, *Providence and Evil*, (1.1), p. 126.

15. *Paradise Lost*, book 12, lines 473–478.

16. The details of the earthquake are taken from Sir James Kendrick, *The Lisbon Earthquake*, London: Methuen 1956. The 'consolatory sermon' is summarized on pp. 81–82, and the story of the Jesuit is told on pp. 87–92.

17. *Gaudium et spes*, § 13.

18. Dostoyevsky, *The Brothers Karamazov*, Harmondsworth: Penguin 1958, book 5, ch. 4, pp. 285–288.

19. The blessed souls in heaven, said Peter the Lombard, see the damned souls suffering in hell and 'are filled not with sorrow but with joy, and give thanks for their own delivery' (*Liber IV Sententiarum*, at the end).

20. From a nineteenth-century Catholic tract called *The Sight of Hell*, written 'for children and young persons'. Quoted in Lecky, *History of European Morals from Augustus to Charlemagne*, London: Longmans 1911, II, pp. 223–224.

21. Albert Camus, *The Plague*, London: Hamish Hamilton 1948, p. 210.

22. Byron, *Cain*, I, 1, 138–140 (spoken by Lucifer).

23. On the principle in general, see Arthur Lovejoy, *The Great Chain of Being*, Harvard University Press 1936. Lovejoy says that the idea was formulated by Plotinus, later used by Augustine and the pseudo-Denis, and was current in the Middle Ages. It was an important element in the Elizabethan world-view (the longest section of E. M. W. Tillyard, *The Elizabethan World Picture*, London: Chatto & Windus 1943 is about this) and it was current in the eighteenth century. Some, including Shakespeare, did not think that this principle explains evil, but rather saw evil as the disruption of the order which the principle expresses.

24. D.-J. Mercier, *Métaphysique générale*, seventh edition, Louvain: Institut supérieur de philosophie 1923, p. 245.

25. See below, p. 61.

26. Paul Ricoeur, *The Symbolism of Evil*, New York: Harper & Row 1967, p. 156.

27. G. C. Berkouwer, *Sin*, Grand Rapids, Michigan: Eerdmans 1971, p. 238.

Chapter 2: Pessimism

1. Shakespeare, *Macbeth*, 5.5.26–28.
2. Voltaire, *Candide*, Harmondsworth: Penguin 1947, ch. 23, p. 110.
3. James Thomson, *The City of Dreadful Night*, section 8.
4. Somerset Maugham, *Of Human Bondage*, London: Heinemann 1937, ch. 106, p. 809.
5. 'The Free Man's Worship' (1903), *The Basic Writings of Bertrand Russell*, London: Allen & Unwin 1961, p. 67.
6. Ricoeur, *The Symbolism of Evil* (1.26), pp. 211–226.
7. U. Ellis-Fermor, *The Frontiers of Drama* (1.9), pp. 141–142.
8. Ibid., p. 70.
9. Marquis de Sade, *Dialogue Between a Priest and a Dying Man*, in *Justine, Philosophy in the Bedroom and Other Writing*, New York: Grove 1965, p. 168.
10. *Justine*, p. 607.
11. Ibid., p. 609.
12. *Philosophy in the Bedroom*, pp. 285–286.
13. *Justine*, p. 608.
14. *Philosophy in the Bedroom*, p. 253.
15. Ibid., p. 254.
16. *Justine*, p. 604.
17. *Juliette*, quoted in Mario Praz, *The Romantic Agony*, second edition, Oxford University Press 1970, ch. 3, § 5, pp. 104–105.
18. *Philosophy in the Bedroom*, p. 272.
19. *Juliette*, quoted in Praz, op. cit., ch. 3, p. 107.
20. Plutarch quotes this from an ancient source of wisdom.
21. James Thomson, *The City of Dreadful Night*, section 16.
22. Ibid., section 14.
23. *The Birth of Tragedy*, Garden City: Doubleday Anchor 1956, end of § 7.
24. 'The Free Man's Worship' (2.5), p. 72.
25. George Steiner makes this remark in *The Death of Tragedy*, London: Faber & Faber 1963, p. 128.
26. D. D. Raphael, *The Paradox of Tragedy*, London: Allen & Unwin 1960, p. 27.
27. Raphael, 'Tragedy and Religion', in Paul S. Saunders (ed.), *Twentieth-Century Interpretations of the Book of Job*, Englewood Cliffs, N.J.: Prentice-Hall 1968, p. 55.
28. Raphael, *The Paradox of Tragedy*, p. 31.

29. Maxwell Anderson, *Winterset,* London: John Lane 1938, near the end, p. 133.

30. William Faulkner, *Absolom, Absolom!* London: Chatto & Windus 1960, ch. 4, p. 127.

31. Albert Camus, *The Rebel,* New York: Vintage Books 1956, p. 5

Part Two: A Moderate Optimism based on Evolution

Chapter 3: Evolutionary Optimism

1. Teilhard de Chardin, *Writings in Time of War,* London: Collins 1968, p. 165; my translation.

2. Teilhard, *The Phenomenon of Man,* London: Collins 1959, p. 51.

3. Teilhard, *The Future of Man,* London: Collins 1964, p. 90.

4. See especially *Adversus Haereses* book 4, ch. 38 p. 1. See also Hick, *Evil and the God of Love* (1.10), p. 202, and J. Bowker, *Problems of Suffering in the Religions of the World,* Cambridge University Press 1970, pp. 84–86. Bowker says that this view was not such a minority view as reading Hick would lead one to think.

5. 'Time', says Charles Vereker, 'was coming to be seen as an essential factor in the process of overcoming evil', *Eighteenth-century Optimism* Liverpool University Press 1967, p. 109, and 'it was time which proved to be the key concept which supported and justified the new optimistic thought' (ibid., p. 149). Lovejoy says that the great development in later eighteenth-century thought was the introduction of time into the Great Chain of Being, *The Great Chain of Being* (1.23), p. 244.

6. Jacques Monod insists that pure chance is not one of several possible hypotheses: 'It is today the *sole* conceivable hypothesis, the only one compatible with observed and tested fact', *Chance and Necessity,* London: Collins 1972, p. 110; see also p. 95 – See also P. McShane, *Randomness, Statistics and Emergence,* Dublin and London: Gill & Macmillan 1970: see index under 'randomness'.

7. Jacques Maritain talks of 'the absolute unforeseeableness of free acts' *Redeeming the Time,* London: Bles 1944, p. 72, and he says that 'the impossibility of being foreseen with absolute certainty' is 'a property of the free act as such', *God and the Permission of Evil,* Milwaukee: Bruce 1960, p. 16. Paul Weiss also maintains that free acts are *de iure* unpredictable, *Man's Freedom,* Yale University Press 1950, pp. 3–8.

8. Maritain says that Bergson wanted 'to safeguard the unforeseeableness of becoming, not only the absolute unforeseeableness of free acts and the relative unforeseeableness of contingent [random?] happenings in the course of nature, but also what he calls the

"radical unforeseeableness" of every moment in the universe. This feeling for unforseeableness', Maritain goes on, 'is a highly philosophic feeling and one which we should not let lie quiescent within us.' (*Redeeming the Time*, p. 72.) Reinhold Niebuhr says: 'In both nature and history each new thing is only one of an infinite number of possibilities which might have emerged at that particular juncture. It is for this reason that, though we can trace a series of causes in retrospect, we can never predict the future with accuracy. There is a profound arbitrariness in every given fact, which rational theories of causation [and, one might add, theological theories of predestination and providence] seek to obscure.' *Beyond Tragedy*, London: Nisbet 1938, p. 8.

Chapter 4: God's Responsibility and Our Own

1. John Hick, *Evil and the God of Love* (1.10), p. 110.
2. Teilhard de Chardin, *Toward the Future*, London: Collins 1975, p. 197.
3. William J. Hill, OP, 'Does God Know the Future? Aquinas and Some Moderns', *Theological Studies*, 36(1975)7.
4. Maritain, *God and the Permission of Evil*, (3.7), p. 16.
5. Maritain, *Existence and the Existent*, Garden City: Image 1956, pp. 122–123.
6. *God and the Permission of Evil*, p. 85.
7. Ps. 139.16–17, *Jerusalem Bible*.
8. Wisd. 8.8, *Jerusalem Bible*.
9. Isa. 46.10, *Jerusalem Bible*.
10. Isa. 48.5, *Jerusalem Bible*.
11. See above p. 7.

Chapter 5: Criticism of Evolutionary Optimism

1. Teilhard de Chardin, *Christianity and Evolution*, London: Collins 1971, p. 82.
2. *Toward the Future* (4.2), pp. 196–197.
3. *Activation of Energy*, London: Collins 1970, p. 259.
4. See Piet Smulders, *The Design of Teilhard de Chardin*, Westminster, Ma.: Newman 1967, pp. 154–155.
5. Vereker says: 'The moral freedom which characterized human sin found no place in the new doctrines. The defect in man which corresponded to sin was that his knowledge of nature and history was confused, disorderly and fragmentary.' *Eighteenth-Century Optimism* (3.5), p. 157.
6. Hick says that World War I 'was to nineteenth-century evolutionary optimisim what the Lisbon earthquake had been to the

eighteenth century doctrine of the best possible world' (*Evil and the God of Love* (1.10), p. 245), but Teilhard was able to cope with it, largely because of his unawareness of the moral evil involved in it; and J.-L. Domenach has remarked on Teilhard's 'failure to recognize any form of political evil other than limitation and absence of universality' ('Le personnalisme de Teilhard de Chardin', *Esprit*, March 1963, p. 353).

7. Quoted in Smulders, *The Design of Teilhard de Chardin*, p. 290. See also C. Mooney, *Teilhard de Chardin and the Mystery of Christ*, London: Collins 1966, pp. 106, 122–145, 208; and Smulders, op. cit., p. 141 and p. 289 n. 42. In 1948 the Jesuit General thought it might be possible for *The Phenomenon of Man* to be published, perhaps with some alterations, without being at once condemned by the Holy Office, and he arranged for Teilhard to visit Rome and meet his critics there face to face. Teilhard seems to have been told that he had overlooked moral evil and the fall, and he wrote 'Some Remarks on the Place and Part of Evil in a World in Evolution'. This, dated Rome, 28 October 1948, now forms an appendix to *The Phenomenon of Man*. Here Teilhard admitted that there might be more disorder in the world that his evolutionary theory accounts for, but he said: 'On this question . . . I do not not feel I am in a position to take a stand.' That was as far as he was prepared to go.

Part Three: Moral Evil: its Nature and Cause

Chapter 6: Moral Evil

1. God, they said, has made man free and autonomous (autexousios). Justin (AD 100–168) said: 'It is not by destiny's law that what man does or suffers happens; each freely does good or evil . . . . God made human beings and angels masters of themselves.' (*Apologia II*, § 7; *PG*, 6,456). Around AD 181, Theophilus of Antioch said that human beings can choose to do good or to do evil, for 'God made man free and autonomous' (*Ad Autolycum*, II, § 27; *PG*, 6.1095).

2. See above, p. 35.

3. Martin Buber, *Good and Evil*, New York: Scribner 1953, p. 88.

4. See L. Monden, *Sin, Liberty and Law*, London: Geoffrey Chapman 1966, p. 38.

5. Karl Menninger, *Whatever Became of Sin?*, London: Hodder & Stoughton 1975, p. 46. Early in his career, Menninger was in effect a determinist and hence did not believe in responsibility, moral evil or guilt. In this late work he proposes 'the revival or reassertion of personal responsibility in all human acts, good and bad. Not total responsibility, but not zero either.' (Ibid., p. 178.) Hence he can now make the assertion in the text above.

6. Peter Berger, *A Rumour of Angels*, Harmondsworth: Pelican 1971, pp. 85–86.

7. See above, p. 7.

8. Dietrich Bonhoeffer, *Ethics*, New York: Macmillan 1965, p. 65. Rearranged edition, SCM Press 1971, p. 47.

Chapter 7: The Content of the Morally Evil Act

1. J. de Finance, for instance, says: 'Hatred for others or for God is only the expression . . . of a love of self, of one's own excellence, of one's own freedom, etc. This love is in itself good, for it is directed towards real values. Only, it is not ruled by reason.' *Connaissance de l'etre*, Paris-Bruges: Desclée de Brouwer 1966, p. 192.

2. Paul Weiss, *Man's Freedom* (3.7), p. 250.

3. 'Must We Burn Sade?', in S. de Beauvoir, *The Marquis de Sade*, London: Calder 1962, p. 70.

4. Karl Barth, *Church Dogmatics*, IV/1, Edinburgh: T. & T. Clark 1956, § 60, p. 399. See also P. Schoonenberg, *Mysterium Salutis*, vol. 2 in the German edition, section on 'Sin as self-destruction'.

5. A. C. Bradley, *Shakespearean Tragedy*, London: Macmillan 1957, p. 301.

6. T. S. Eliot, *Murder in the Cathedral*, London: Faber & Faber 1938, chorus in part 2, p. 68.

7. See Aquinas, *Summa Theologica*, 1–2, 29, 34.

8. Georges Bernanos, *Diary of a Country Priest*, London: Bodley Head 1937, p. 314.

9. D. H. Lawrence, *Women in Love*, London: Heinemann Phoenix 1954, ch. 23, p. 301.

10. E. Fromm, *The Art of Loving*, London: Allen & Unwin 1957, p. 60.

11. D. H. Lawrence, *Lady Chatterley's Lover*, Harmondsworth: Penguin 1960, ch. 13, p. 200.

12. Choderlos de Laclos, *Les liaisons dangereuses*, 6th letter.

13. Ibid., 70th letter.

14. See the 125th letter.

15. Maurice Blanchot, 'Sade', in Sade, *Justine etc.* (2.9), p. 40.

16. Ibid., p. 55.

17. Byron, *Lara*, canto I, lines 347–348.

18. T. S. Eliot, *The Cocktail Party*, London: Faber & Faber, 1950 Act I scene 3, p. 99.

19. Sartre, *No Exit*, near the end of the play.

20. Camus, *The Fall*, London: Hamish Hamilton 1957, p. 76.

21. A. de Saint-Exupéry, *The Wisdom of the Sands*, London: Hollis & Carter 1952, ch. 113. p. 311.

22. Schoonenberg says: 'Sin is not only a rebellion against valid norms, but also the refusal to collaborate in elaborating other norms. The "hardness of heart" (Mark 10.5; Matt. 19.8) which in Judaism (and also in paganism) prevented the indissolubility of marriage, is an example of a sin which worked against the establishment of a norm, even if Jesus . . . represented it as the rejection of a norm which had been in existence "from the beginning".' *Mysterium Salutis*, French edition Paris: Cerf 1970, vol. 8, p. 19.

23. *Macbeth*, 3.2.49.

24. In *The Rebel* (2.31), Camus emphasizes that noble revolt stems from a prior acceptance (p. 16 and elsewhere).

25. L. Lavelle says: 'At the heart of freedom there is an act of acceptance, a yes which we say to being and to life. . . . This yes is always present deep within us, even when we refuse to formulate it.' *Les puissances du moi*, Paris: Flammarion 1948, pp. 151–152.

26. *Paradise Lost*, book 9, lines 129–130.

27. *Faust*, part I, in the study.

28. *Juliette*, quoted in Praz, *The Romantic Agony* (2.17), ch. 3, p. 107, and above, p. 20.

29. *Justine*, quoted in Praz, op. cit., p. 107.

30. *Partage de midi*, in Paul Claudel, *Théatre*, Paris: Gallimard Pléiade, 1956, I, 1116.

31. Quoted in H. Küng, *Justification*, New York: Thomas Nelson 1964, ch. 23, p. 147.

32. Ulrich Simon, *The Theology of Auschwitz*, London: Gollancz 1967, p. 88.

33. Dietrich Bonhoeffer, *Ethics* (6.8), pp. 105–106; rearranged edition p. 85.

34. E. Fromm, *The Anatomy of Human Destructiveness*, New York: Holt, Rinehart & Winston 1973, p. 100.

35. Ibid., p. 186.

36. Mercier, *Métaphysique générale* (1.24), p. 245.

37. William Temple, *Nature, Man and God*, London: Macmillan 1956, p. 362.

38. Ricoeur, *The Symbolism of Evil* (1.26), pp. 116–117.

39. *Macbeth*, 1.4.151.

40. Ibid., 1.5.40–54.

41. *Titus Andronicus*, 5.1.125–131.

42. Helen Gardner, *Religion and Literature*, London: Faber & Faber 1971, p. 49.

43. *Paradise Lost*, book 4, line 110.

44. *The Brothers Karamazov* (1.18), book 3, ch. 4, p. 124.

45. Ibid., book 11, ch. 3, p. 682.

46. 'The Black Cat' in *Tales of Mystery and Imagination*.

47. *Lautréamont's Maldoror*, London: Allison & Busby 1970, pp. 66, 75.

48. In recent years there has been an explosion of books, articles and films about the occult, and there may have been an increase in the practice of witchcraft. Much of the practice is probably play-acting of a rather nasty kind, and for the most part the books are bought by people seeking the sort of thrill one obtains from Gothic novels, but there may be an element of serious devotion to evil in the craze.

49. Karl Heim, *Jesus the World's Perfecter*, Edinburgh & London: Oliver & Boyd 1959, p. 60.

50. Karl Barth, *Church Dogmatics* (7.4), IV/1, § 60, p. 419.

51. Ibid., p. 437.

52. Karl Heim, *Jesus the Lord*, Edinburgh & London: Oliver & Boyd 1959, p. 106.

53. A. Vergote, 'La peine dans la dialectique de l'innocence, de la transgression et de la reconciliation', *Le mythe de la peine*, Paris: Aubier 1967, p. 398.

Chapter 8: The Mystery of Evil

1. See above, p. 13.

2. Emil Brunner, *Man in Revolt*, London: Lutterworth 1939, p. 130.

3. Hick, *Evil and the God of Love* (1.10), pp. 62–63.

4. Ricoeur, *The Symbolism of Evil* (1.26), p. 155. See also K. Jung, *Aion Collected Works*, vol. 9, part 2; New York: Pantheon 1959, most of ch. 5, especially pp. 41–62.

5. Sir. 15.11–12, *Jerusalem Bible*.

6. *Homilia I de proditione Judae* § 3, *PG*, 49,377.

7. Augustine, *On Free Will*, 1.11 § 21.

8. Ibid., 1.16 § 34.

9. Ibid., 3.1 § 2.

10. Ibid., 3.17 § 48.

11. Ibid., 3.17 § 49.

12. Ibid., 3.22 § 63.

13. Kant, *Religion Within the Limits of Reason Alone*, New York: Harper Torchbook 1960. p. 17.

14. Ibid., p. 24.

15. Ibid., p. 40.

16. Ricoeur says that at an early stage of man's moral development doing wrong is thought to consist in violating some objective, exterior rule, and it results in defilment; but 'the consciousness of guilt consitutes a veritable revolution in the experience of evil: that

which is primary is no longer the reality of defilement, the objective violation of the Interdict, or the Vengeance let loose by the violation, but the evil use of liberty, felt as an internal diminution of the value of the self.' *The Symbolism of Evil* (1.26), p. 102.

17. Maritain, *God and the Permission of Evil* (3.7), pp. 21, 45–46; *St Thomas and the Problem of Evil*, Milwaukee: Marquette University Press 1942, pp. 22–36.

18. *God and the Permission of Evil*, p. 21. Lonergan proposes substantially the same view: 'By basic sin I shall mean the failure of free will to choose a morally obligatory course of action or its failure to reject a morally reprehensible course of action. . . . If he [a person] wills, he does what he ought; if he wills he diverts his attention from proposals to do what he ought not; but if he fails to will, then the obligatory course of action is not executed; again, if he fails to will, his attention remains on illicit proposals; the incompleteness of their intelligibility and the incoherence of their apparent reasonableness are disregarded; and in this contraction of consciousness, which is the basic sin, there occurs the wrong action.' *Insight*, London: Longmans 1957, p. 666. [reissued Darton, Longman & Todd 1978].

19. Hick, *Evil and the God of Love* (1.10), pp. 68–69.

20. Ibid., p. 180.

21. Ibid., pp. 285–286.

22. Fromm, *The Anatomy of Human Destructiveness* (7.34), pp. 259–260, 226–227.

23. *Catechesis IV*, § 20; *PG*, 33,481.

24. *Adversus Haereses*, 4.37 § 2; *PG*, 7.1100.

25. Kant, *Religion Within the Limits of Reason Alone* (8.13), p. 36.

26. See above, p. 52, especially the quotation from de Finance in ch. 7, footnote 1.

27. P. Schoonenberg, *Man and Sin*, Notre Dame University Press, Press 1965, p. 20.

28. Joseph Rickaby, 'The Greek Doctrine of Necessity: a Speculation on the Origin of Evil', quoted in Hick, *Evil and the God of Love* (1.10), p. 268.

29. Maritain, *St Thomas and the Problem of Evil* (8.17), p. 6.

30. Teilhard de Chardin, *Christianity and Evolution* (5.1), p. 195; see also the appendix to *The Phenomenon of Man* (3.2).

31. See above, pp. 25–26.

32. C. S. Lewis, *The Problem of Pain*, London: Geoffrey Bles 1940, pp. 72–73.

33. Helen Gardner, *Religion and Literature* (7.42), pp. 48–49.

34. Julius Müller, *The Christian Doctrine of Sin*, Edinburgh: T. & T. Clark 1877, II, 173–174.

35. Barth, *Church Dogmatics* (7.4), IV/1, § 60, p. 433.
36. Brunner, *The Mediator*, London: Lutterworth 1934, p. 124.
37. Brunner, *Man in Revolt* (8.2), p. 132.
38. Austin Farrer, *Love Almighty and Ills Unlimited*, London: Collins 1962, p. 140. See also ch. 5, 'The Riddle of Sin', of Berkouwer, *Sin* (1.27).
39. Kant, *Religion Within the Limits of Reason Alone* (8.13), p. 38.
40. N. Berdyaev, *Freedom and the Spirit*, London: Geoffrey Bles 1935, p. 163.
41. V. Jankélévitch, *Le pardon*, Paris: Aubier 1967, p. 92.
42. Ibid., p. 207.
43. Bernard Lonergan, *Insight* (8.18), p. 667.
44. See below, pp. 109–11.
45. Barth, *Church Dogmatics* (7.4), IV/1, § 60, p. 410.
46. Hick, *Evil and the God of Love* (1.10), pp. 324–325.
47. Quoted in Vereker, *Eighteenth-Century Optimism* (3.5), p. 296.
48. Farrer, *Love Almighty and Ills Unlimited* (8.38), p. 151. See also Fromm, *The Anatomy of Human Destructiveness* (7.34), p. 4.
49. Georges Bernanos, *Joy*, London: The Catholic Book Club 1949, part 1, ch. 4, p. 98.

Chapter 9: God and Sin

1. See above, p. 35.
2. See above, pp. 35f.
3. Ricoeur says, 'The etiological myth of Adam is the most extreme attempt to separate the origin of evil from the origin of the good; its intention is to set up a *radical* origin of evil distinct from the more *primordial* origin of the goodness of things. . . . [It] makes man a *beginning* of evil in the bosom of a creation which has already had its absolute *beginning* in the creative act of God.' *The Symbolism of Evil* (1.26), p. 233.
4. Sir. 15.11, *Jerusalem Bible*.
5. *Oratio catechetica magna*, ch. 5 ad finem; *PG*, 45,25.
6. Barth, *Church Dogmatics* (7.4), IV/1, § 60, p. 409.
7. Maritain, *God and the Permission of Evil* (3.7), p. 1n.
8. Ibid., p. 6.
9. Ibid., p. 112.
10. Ibid., p. 10.
11. *Freedom in the Modern World* London: Sheed & Ward 1935, p. 27.
12. *God and the Permission of Evil*, pp. 79–80.
13. Ibid., p. 85.
14. Journet, *The Meaning of Evil* (1.13), p. 178. Journet seems to

be having things both ways when he says this, but elsewhere says that God lets people sin when the sin fits in with his plan (see above, p. 8).

15. See above, p. 33.

16. Albert Camus, *The Rebel* (2.31), p. 56.

17. D. D. Raphael, 'Tragedy and Religion' (2.27), p. 55.

18. J. L. Mackie, 'Evil and Omnipotence', *Mind*, 64(1955)209. It is to be noted that in the first sentence it is established that something is not *logically* impossible, and then in the second sentence it is regarded as a practical possibility, as if logical impossibility were the only kind of inherent impossibility. See above, p. 24.

19. Anthony Flew, 'Compatibilism, Free Will and God', *Philosophy*, 48(1973)233.

Chapter 10 : The Wages of Sin and the Thesis of this Book

1. II Peter 2.12, *Jerusalem Bible*.

2. *Richard III*, 5.3.188–201.

3. Albert Camus, *The Rebel*, (2.31), op. 186.

4. *Macbeth*, 2.3.94–95.

5. Ibid., 5.5.24–28.

6. Brunner, *Man in Revolt* (8.2), p. 255.

7. *Macbeth*, 5.3.22–26.

8. Bernanos, *Joy* (8.49), part 2, ch. 3, p. 85.

9. Karl Rahner, *Spiritual Exercises* New York: Herder & Herder 1965, p. 52.

10. See above, p. 24.

11. *Macbeth*, 3.2.23.

12. Camus, *The Rebel* (2.31), p. 281. Camus says that this is so 'if the world has no higher meaning, if man is only responsible to man', but this condition is unnecessary.

13. William Faulkner, *Requiem for a Nun*, London: Chatto & Windus 1965, act 2 scene 1, p. 145.

14. *Macbeth*, 4.2.73–75.

15. *Troilus and Cressida*, 1.3.116–126.

16. T. S. Eliot, *Murder in the Cathedral* (7.6), chorus, p. 77.

17. T. S. Eliot, *The Family Reunion*, London: Faber & Faber 1963, part 2, scene 1, pp. 85–86.

18. Milton, *Paradise Lost*, book 9, lines 781–784.

19. Ibid., lines 1000–1001.

20. Peter de Rosa says: 'When we sin against God the change and the loss are entirely in *us*. . . . The loss is all on our side; we suffer the injury and not he. This is what it means to offend or injure God: to be responsible for a situation in which we suffer dreadfully.' *God our*

Saviour, London: Geoffrey Chapman 1968, p. 96.

21. *Richard III*, 4.2.63–64.

22. *Macbeth*. 3.2.55. The sense of the line is that, having begun by murder, Macbeth will strengthen his position by more evil deeds.

23. Ibid., 3.4.136–138.

24. Aeschylus, *Agamemnon*, translated by Richard Lattimore, University of Chicago Press 1953, lines 758–760.

25. Bernanos, *Un crime*, Paris: Plan 1935, near the end of part I.

26. Augustine, *De Genesi ad litteram*, imperfectus liber, 1 § 3.

27. See above, pp. 40–42.

28. C. S. Lewis, *The Problem of Pain* (8.32), p. 77. Hugh Silvester quotes Lewis and then himself puts the figure at 95 per cent *Arguing With God*, Downer's Grove, Ill.: Inter-Varsity Press 1972, pp. 32–33.

29. F. D. E. Schleiermacher, *The Christian Faith*, Edinburgh: T. & T. Clark 1928, § 48, p. 185.

30. Ibid., § 75, p. 316.

31. Barth, *Church Dogmatics* (7.4), III/3, § 50, p. 310.

32. Loc. cit. See also Brunner (8.2), p. 115, and G. A. Buttrick, *God, Pain and Evil*, Nashville: Abingdon 1966, pp. 32–33.

Part Four: The Remedy for Moral Evil

Chapter 11: Repentance

1. Faulkner, *Requiem for a Nun* (10.13), act 1 scene 3, p. 85.

2. T. S. Eliot, *The Family Reunion* (10.17), part 1 scene 1, p. 27.

3. Sade, 'Dialogue Between a Priest and a Dying Man' (2.9), p. 174.

4. Sade, *Justine* (2.10), p. 696.

5. See above, pp. 63–64.

6. See above, p. 47.

7. Max Scheler says: 'But what may Repentance accomplish in its attack upon guilt? Two things – of which it alone, and nothing else, is capable. It cannot drive out of the world the external natural [objective] reality of the deed and its causal consequences, nor the evil character which the deed acquires *ipso facto*. All that stays in the world. But it can totally kill and extinguish the reactive effect of the deed within the human soul [subjectivity], and with it the root of an eternity of renewed guilt and evil. Repentance, at least in its perfect form, genuinely annihilates the psychic quality called "guilt".' *On the Eternal in Man* London: SCM Press 1960, p. 55; this quotation is continued below, p. 126.

8. Ibid., p. 50.

9. Ibid., pp. 51–52.

10. Ibid., p. 36.

11. Ibid., p. 42.

12. Ibid., pp. 42–43.

13. Ibid., pp. 55–56 (this is a continuation of the quotation in footnote 7 above).

Chapter 12: Forgiveness

1. In this chapter I am particularly indebted to Vladimir Jankélévitch, from whose *Le pardon* (8.41) I shall frequently quote.

2. See above, pp. 70–72.

3. See above, p. 72.

4. See above, pp. 63–64, 98.

5. *Nostra Aetate*, § 3.

6. Jankélévitch, *Le pardon*, p. 79. He fairly clearly has in mind the evils of Nazi Germany.

7. Jer. 36.3, *Jerusalem Bible*.

8. Max Scheler, *Formalism in Ethics and Non-Formal Ethics of Values*, Evanston: Northwestern University Press 1973, p. 365.

9. Journet, *The Meaning of Evil* (1.13), p. 209.

10. John G. McKenzie, *Guilt*, London: Allen & Unwin 1962, p. 179.

11. Jankélévitch, *Le pardon*, p. 145.

12. Ibid., p. 110.

13. Ibid., p. 124.

14. Ibid., pp. 141–143.

15. Ibid., p. 139.

16. Ibid., pp. 89–90.

17. 'Le pardon, à vrai dire, ne nous demande pas de sacrifier le tout de notre être-propre' (Ibid., p. 157).

18. I said this myself in *Love and the Person*, London: Geoffrey Chapman 1967, pp. 147–148.

19. Karl Jaspers, *Philosophy*, Chicago University Press 1970, II, 241–242.

20. Jankélévitch, *Traité des vertus*, Paris: Bordas 1949, p. 465.

21. Faulkner, *Requiem for a Nun* (10.13), act 2 scene 1, p. 138.

22. See above, p. 47.

INDEX

Absurdity, 83
Acceptance, 38, 55, 100, 116
Action, vii, 38
Adam, 6, 8, 67, 77, 87, 88, 117f., 127
Aeschylus, 90, 129
Alienation, 53, 83, 86f., 103
Ambrose, 117
Amoral behaviour, 45f.
Anderson, Maxwell, 120
Anger, vii, 80
Anti-creation, 79
Aquinas, St Thomas, 13, 52, 64, 123
Art, 6, 12, 18
Augustine, St, 8, 13, 62, 91f., 118, 125, 129

Barth, Karl, viii, 52, 57, 60, 70, 72, 78, 94, 123, 125, 127, 129
Baudelaire, 15
Beauvoir, Simone de, 52, 123
Being, 13, 20, 55, 57, 87
Berdyaev, N., 71, 127
Berger, Peter, 48, 123
Berkouwer, G. C., 13, 119
Bernanos, G., 52, 73, 84, 91, 123, 127, 128, 129

Bible, 3, 7, 8, 36, 46, 58, 78, 79, 80, 84, 92
Blanchot, M., 123
Bonhoeffer, Dietrich, 57, 123, 124
Bowker, John, 120
Bradley, A. C., 52, 123
Brunner, Emil, 71, 125, 127, 128, 129
Buber, Martin, 48, 122
Buttrick, G. A., 129
Byron, 129

Camus, Albert, 11, 20, 54, 80, 83, 86, 118, 120, 123, 124, 128
Chance, 3, 6, 29, 30
Charity, 6
Christianity, 5, 19, 20, 27, 73, 80, 91
Claudel, Paul, 56, 124
Commitment, 85
Conscience, 7, 82
Creation, 35f., 42, 46, 77, 81, 94, 127
Cruelty, 17, 58, 73
Cyril of Jerusalem, 66

Darkness, 13, 52, 55, 61, 62, 70, 73, 93

Darwin, Charles, 28
Death, viii, 6, 82, 85, 91
Demonic, 72
Design, 9, 14
Destruction, 56f., 60, 67, 69, 73,
    79, 82, 87, 89
Determinism, 29, 30f., 122
Devil, viii, 73
Disorder, *see* Unorder
Domenach, J.-L., 122
Dostoyevsky, F., viii, 118

Eliot, T. S., 123, 128, 129
Ellis-Fermoe, U., 15, 117, 119
Ethics, 17
Evil, vii, 5, 8, 12, 13, 15, 17, 28,
    39, 48, 50, 55, 57ff., 62ff.,
    71, 75f., 80, 93, 98, 101,
    103, 115, 118, 122, 124, 125,
    127, 129
  moral, vii, 7, 13, 40f., 45–50,
    54, 61, 63ff., 69ff., 89f., 122
  physical, vii, 42, 93
  problem of, vii, 39, 98
  See also Morally evil act,
    Mystery of evil
Evolution, vii, 25ff., 30, 35, 40,
    69, 70, 73, 85, 93, 122
Evolutionary optimism, 23–30,
    34, 39–42
Existence-span, 23

Fall, 6, 18, 70, 87, 91, 92, 122
  Fortunate Fall, 6, 117
Farrer, Austin, 71, 73, 127
Fate, 46
Faulkner, William, 87, 98, 113,
    120, 128, 129, 130
Fear, 84, 100
Flew, Anthony, 81, 128
Foreknowledge, 34f., 76f., 81,
    120f.
Forgiveness, viii, 7, 68, 72, 103–
    115, 116

Freedom, 32, 36f., 53, 62f., 70,
    83, 101, 112, 120, 122f.
Free will, 24, 29, 33, 37, 46, 63f.,
    66, 69, 127
  Free Will Defence, 80f.
Friendship, 85, 103, 108
Fromm, E., 52, 57, 66, 123, 124,
    126

Gardner, Helen, 59, 124, 126
Geach, Peter, 4, 8, 117, 118
Generosity, 111
God, 3ff., 6f., 8, 10f., 15, 17, 31f.,
    34ff., 46, 60, 68, 70, 74, 75–
    81, 87, 89, 113, 115, 122
    128
  will of, 3, 7, 8ff., 34, 37f., 75ff.
Good, 8, 13, 34, 38, 55, 57f.,
    64f., 67, 75, 89, 93, 122, 127
Gregory of Nyssa, 78
Grace, 91, 111
Guilt, viii, 7, 46, 90, 98f., 102,
    107, 122, 129

Heim, Karl, 125
Hell, 10f., 54
Hick, John, 31, 62, 65f., 72, 117,
    120, 121f., 125, 126, 127
Hill, William, 35, 121
Hitler, A., 76
Hope, 101
Hostility, 87
Huxley, T. H., 73

Illusion, 5
Impossibility, 24
  inherent, 24, 31, 69, 128
  logical, 24, 80, 128
Incarnation, 73, 118
Irenaeus, 28

Jankélévitch, V., 71, 104, 106,
    110, 112, 127, 130
Jaspers, K., 112, 117, 130

Jenyns, Soames, 4, 117
Jesus, viii, 37, 60, 83, 124
Journet, C., 8, 79, 107, 118, 127f., 130
Justice, 10, 110f.

Kant, I., 63, 66, 71, 125, 126, 127
Kierkegaard, S., 84
Küng, H., 124

Lavelle, L., 124
Lawrence, D. H., 123
Lewis, C. S., 70, 93, 126, 129
Light, 13, 55, 61, 93
Lonergan, B., 72, 126, 127
Love, 85, 103, 108f., 110, 112ff., 123
Lovejoy, A., 117, 118, 120

Mackenzie, John G., 107, 130
Mackie, J. L., 128
Manicheans, 13
Maritain, J., 36, 64f., 69, 78f., 120f.
Maugham, Somerset, 14, 119
Meaninglessness, 14f., 19, 83
Menninger, K., 48, 119
Mercier, D.-J., 58, 118, 125
Milton, John, 4, 8, 56, 59, 128
Molinist theory, 76
Monden, L., 68, 122
Monod, Jacques, 120
Mooney, C., 122
Moral obligation, 45ff.
Morality, 20
Morally evil act, viii, 48, 51–60, 62, 67, 75
Morally good act, 49
Müller, Julius, 70, 126
Mystery, 73f.
    of evil, 61–74, 75, 79, 82, 93, 98f.

Nature, 15ff., 40, 56, 70, 88, 93

Necessity, 29, 46, 69f.
Niebuhr, Reinhold, 121
Nietzsche, F., 18

Omnipotence, viii, 31, 36, 80, 116
Omniscience, viii, 36
Optimism, 3–13, 15, 27f., 38, 69
Order, 20, 24, 73
Outsiderhood, 53, 86, *see also* Alienation

Pain, 6, 24, 111
Paul, 72, 79, 84, 91
Peace, 84, 116
Pessimism, 14–20, 38
Plato, 28
Plotinus, 13, 28, 118
Plutarch, 119
Poe, Edgar Alan, 59
Pope, Alexander, 4
Prayer, petitionary, 7, 38
Praz, Mario, 119
Principle of Plenitude, 12
Probability, 29, 30
Process theology, vii
Progress, 25, 26f., 69, 73
Providence, viii, 6, 116
Punishment, viii, 11, 75, 91, 109

Rahner, Karl, 84, 128
Random events, 28ff., 120
Raphael, D. D., 80, 119f., 128
Reality, 55f., 68, 87
Reason, 55, 74, 83, 123
Reconciliation, 7, 107, 114
Redemption, 7, 83
Regret, 46, 100
Repentance, viii, 7, 97–102, 107f., 111, 113, 116, 129
Respect, 53f., 86
Responsibility, 31–38, 46, 49, 62f., 65, 67, 75, 77, 101, 122, 128

Resurrection, viii
Revenge, 84, 100f., 111
Rickaby, Joseph, 69, 126
Ricoeur, Paul, 13, 15, 58, 62, 62, 119, 124, 125f., 127
Right, 6, 45, 81, 88, 113
Rise theory, 28, 92
de Rosa, Peter, 128
Rousseau, 92
Russell, Bertrand, 14, 18, 119

Sade, Marquis de, 15f., 53, 56, 59, 76, 98, 119, 129
Sadness, 84
Saint Exupery, A. de, 54, 123
Salvation, 7, 83
Sartre, J.-P., 123
Scheler, Max, 100f., 107, 129, 130
Schleiermacher, F. D. E., 93, 129
Schoonenberg, Piet, 124, 126
Self-love, 52, 123
Sertillanges, A.-D., 5, 69, 117
Shadows, 93, 94
Shakespeare, William, viii, 15, 20, 58f., 70, 82, 89, 118f.
Shame, 100
Sickness, vii, 84f.
Simon, U., 124
Sin, viii, 7, 8, 41, 42, 50, 52, 57, 60f., 64, 67, 68ff., 72, 73, 75–81, 82–94, 98, 103, 107, 115, 121, 122, 123f., 126, 128

Smith, Adam, 100
Smulders, Piet, 121f.
Spiritual growth, 6
Standenmaier, F. A., 57
Steiner, G., 119
Suffering, 5, 6, 25, 26f., 32, 38, 39f., 42, 69, 82, 85, 89, 93, 104, 111, 113, 128

Teilhard de Chardin, P., vii, 27f., 31, 39ff., 69, 70, 92f., 120, 121f., 126
Temple, William, 58, 124
Theophilus of Antioch, 122
Thomson, James, 14, 119
Tillyard, E. M. W., 118
Time, 120
Tragedy, 5, 7, 18f., 20, 80, 113
Trinity, 73

Unorder, vii, 24, 34, 38, 39f., 70, 73, 75

Value, 47, 55, 112, 125
Vereker, Charles, 120, 121
Vergote, A., 60, 125
Voltaire, 5, 119

Waste, 5, 6, 26, 41, 80
Weiss, Paul, 52, 120, 123
Will, 32ff., 55, 56f., 61, 63f., 73, 75, 89, 98ff., 105, 126
Work, 38, 116
Wrong, 45, 47, 64, 69, 75, 76, 81, 88, 98, 113, 125